BUSY MOM'S

CHEAT SHEET

RAISING HAPPY HEALTHY KIDS

LILLY CADOCH

PICKI BELI PUBLISHING
NEW YORK, NEW YORK

D0377739

Lilly Cadoch/Picki Beli Publishing
P.O. Box 388
Oceanside, New York 11572
www.busymomscheatsheet.com

Book Layout ©2013 BookDesignTemplates.com

Ordering Information:
Quantity sales. Special discounts are available on quantity purchases by corporations, associations, and others. For details, contact the "Special Sales Department" at the address above.

Busy Mom's Cheat Sheet/ Lilly Cadoch. —1st ed.
ISBN 978-0-9969633-0-5

Library of Congress Control Number: 2015956620

CONTENTS

To my children, Natanel and Itai, for letting me experience the kind of love I never dreamt existed before I had you boys.

To my soulmate, Eli, for believing that I can do anything I set my mind to and supporting me every step of the way.

"Food is a gateway to a much better life–fueling our bodies so that we can fuel our dreams."

—Kris Carr

[1]

Introduction

My story dates back to when I was almost eight years old. My father passed away from cancer before his 34th birthday, and from the day I lost him, the childhood I had known was over. My mother was left with no financial security, three children to raise, and a lot of heart-ache. As the oldest of the three, I took on the role of raising my younger sister and brother. My mom had to work long hours, seven days a week, just to make ends meet. Watching her struggle, I made it my mission to become an independent woman who wouldn't have to rely on a man to take care of me. I knew a big part of achieving that independence meant getting a good education, something my mom never had the opportunity to receive. I put my youth and the fun that should have come with it aside, making school work my number one priority. The focus on education paid off, allowing me to graduate high school with 4.2 GPA, followed by a 3.8 GPA and honors when I graduated from UC Berkeley with a psychology degree. My academic success allowed me to secure a job at a prestigious consulting company six months before graduating. I felt like I had finally achieved my goal: I was able to support myself without depending on anyone.

Fast forward 20 years. I continued to climb up the corporate ladder in several different jobs on my way to reach financial freedom and seemed to do very well. One would think that with all of my successes, I would have felt confident and able. But I didn't. I felt like a fraud. I always thought it was a matter of time until someone found out I didn't know what I was doing. I was afraid they would ask me to do something at work I didn't know how to do. I never had the internal confidence to be ready to face any situation, regardless if I was prepared or not.

Looking back on everything, I can now say it was because I was never really taught about the value of self-worth and self-appreciation. I wasn't given the support or praise I needed to establish a feeling of confidence in myself. I attributed any successes I accomplished to outside forces or just being lucky. I figured that anything I accomplished that came from working hard was due to pure luck, instead of realizing that who I was as a person along with my intelligence played a huge role in how things worked out for me. I internalized my failures and found myself afraid to take on challenges that I wasn't 100% sure I would succeed in. I wasn't interested in taking risks and I was afraid of change.

Now, being older and wiser and a mom myself, I no longer fault my mother for the struggles I faced. I can look back and understand that she did the best she could. I actually credit her for teaching me perseverance and how to work hard to provide for my family even during tough times.

The journey of trying to teach myself all the things I never learned as a kid has been long and challenging. I've learned that failure and success are joined together on the same path and one cannot exist without the other. I've learned that the ones who truly fail are the ones who end up giving up too early. I've learned that just because I feel fear doesn't mean I should stop moving forward. Feel the fear and do it anyway. I've learned that self-love combined with a healthy lifestyle, such as eating healthy food, exercise, and sleep were just a few more things that can add to my success and happiness. Having these experiences and successfully learning from them made me want to help my kids and all kids by sharing my life lessons.

In today's global economy, more is expected of our kids than ever before. To have a better chance for a successful future, our kids are expected to perform from a very young age. They are taking more standardized tests than we can count, expected to excel at competitive sports, participate in extracurricular activities, all while excelling academically in their coursework. Not only that but college admissions are getting more and more difficult, with no guarantee of getting into the college of choice. As a result, we expect a lot from our kids for them to succeed.

Our goal as parents is to make sure our kids are provided with the optimal conditions in which to succeed. One of our responsibilities is to ensure our kids are eating healthy. This starts with the food we provide them. But our food supply is getting worse every day, which is only working against us. Our kids are eating more processed foods and sugar than ever before, and not enough fruits and vegetables. We live in a country where they count ketchup as a vegetable in the school lunch program and where we are not always told what is in our food supply. According to Food Chemical News, the leading news service on US food law and policy, a U.S. Senate appropriations bill also stipulates that "tomato paste used to make pizzas can be counted toward the weekly total of vegetable servings." The childhood obesity rate is at an all-time high, leading to more cases of childhood diabetes than our medical system is prepared for. It is a very sad fact that this might be the first generation that our kids' lifespan is expected to be shorter than ours, even by five years.

That is why we need to arm our kids with the physical, emotional and mental tools so that they have a better shot at figuring out their life-path and achieving their goals. A part of arming our kids with this knowledge means that we need to communicate to our children that a healthy life starts with a healthy body. A strong body leads to a strong mind. An open, calm mind helps us discover our life's purpose. Providing these tools to our loved ones is no easy feat considering we are already very busy caregivers. We have so much going on and adding more items to our ever growing to-do list could be enough to throw us over the edge. That coupled with the fact that the food system isn't really in our favor and most of the food options out there are not really good for us.

The simple truth is that it is hard to find the right work-life balance where you feel you are giving everything your all. Most of my days are about getting through the day and making sure everyone has what they need, and never asking myself what I need.

While I am a parent who is devoted to her children, I have a ton going on and struggle with things such as what to feed my kids for dinner, what to pack for school lunch, what snacks they should have, and how to make my morning routine easier. I think about how I can be present with my kids without doing ten other things when they need my attention; having patience, giving each child the kind of attention they need, setting limits yet staying close to them; and having to be five places at once and feeding everyone foods that they like that are both easy and healthy. If any of these challenges ring a bell, I hear you!

After giving birth to my two sons, I vowed to teach them all the lessons I had struggled to learn. This book is my public guide to my boys and to any other parent out there dedicated to ensuring that their children have a better life than they ever did. I brought two children into this world with the hope that they are as prepared as possible to have a successful life. Giving them these tools to have a healthy body, mind and spirit will give them a head start in achieving their goals and fulfilling their dreams. Beyond my own children, my wish is that all kids have the opportunity to learn how to have a healthy body, a nourished mind and a peaceful spirit.

I've started to introduce the concepts in this book to my family and I am already seeing how it's helped my husband and my kids prosper. It is my wish for my children, and all other children, to be exposed to all these tools early in life so that they can have a head start on their future and a better shot for happiness and success. It has been said that happiness is not about the things you have, but of the legacy you leave behind.

It took me over 40 years to learn this myself. While the old ad-age "better late than never," is true, I really feel that if I learned these tools when I was growing up, I would have saved myself a lot of heart-aches, self-doubt, anxiety and depression. I would have felt better about myself, looked better, had more confidence in myself and my ability to take on new challenges and perhaps find my life's passion earlier in life. I've seen first-hand the difference incorporating these principles in my life has made. My hope is that when you read this book that you will have some "aha" moments on things you too wished you learned growing up and that you feel inspired to teach your children so that they don't have to wait as long as you did.

In this book, I break down these pearls of wisdom into three categories: Body, Mind, and Spirit. This trifecta makes up our entire being and if any of them get out of balance, it can throw everything out of whack. It is important to address body first as your body is the foundation that needs to be solid in order to have the proper capacity to handle the mind and spirit. Not only does our food feed our cells, it also feeds our mind, our thoughts, and our soul, so starting with the food we eat is the most logical first step. When we have a healthy body, we can more clearly tackle our mind and spiritual needs.

[2]

Body

You only have one body in this lifetime. Bodies are amazing and so good to us. They take each breath without us having to ask. Our hearts beat without us thinking about it. Our stomach digests food and provides nutrients to our body without us even noticing. However, because our bodies give us all of these things subtly and selflessly, we often forget to thank our bodies for all that they do. We take all these things for granted until we get sick or hurt. We need to treat our body as our sacred temple and be very selective about what we put into it. Unfortunately, that is easier said than done. In this day and age, we often don't know or even understand what is really in our food supply. We are inundated with deceptive marketing messages and it's increasingly difficult to navigate the shopping aisles.

In this section, I will demystify the process of identifying and understanding food labels so you may start to understand the impact of certain ingredients in your body and your kids' bodies, a process that will lead you to feel confident about knowing what is in our food supply and what you are putting in your mouth and your children's mouth. Then I will shed light on the importance of getting a good night's sleep and I'll discuss how exercise not only nourishes your body but also your mind. At the end of this section, I will list creative ways to incorporate exercise into your family lifestyle.

Before we start, I want to make you aware of my 80/20 rule. It is my belief that it is not feasible or realistic to incorporate and follow all the tools you would learn here 100% of the time. And that is OK. It's important to have balance: to live fully and to splurge at times. I personally strive to incorporate these tools 80% of the time. Some weeks I do more, while other weeks, when I have a lot going on, I may do less. But rather than give up, I acknowledge the reasons I wasn't able to do X, Y, and Z and try to get closer to that 80% the following week without beating myself up. After all, we are only humans, not robots!

Now that we have 80/20 out of the way, let's jump in. This section is broken down into six lessons about how to nourish our bodies. Had I known these six lessons growing up, my life would have gone very differently. I wouldn't have struggled with my weight while putting my body through the abuse of a "yo-yo" cycle of fad diets.

I'll never forget how in eighth grade, one of my close friends and I, wanting to lose weight quickly and easily, stole a couple of my aunt's prescription diet pills from her medicine cabinet. The 24 hours that ensued were terrifying. I felt like my heart was beating so fast that I was afraid I would have a heart attack. And at the same time, I was too scared to tell my mom what I did for fear I would get in trouble. If I had the tools to eat right, I wouldn't have felt the need to take such foolish risks.

I know that on occasion you and your family will eat your junk food of choice (I personally have a weakness for Doritos and ice cream). You will let your kids stay up late, and your family may go through an exercise lull when things get super busy. Hopefully, after reading this book, you will do so consciously, sparingly, and with full knowledge of the effects. My goal is to replace the guilt and anxiety so many of us experience, with easy to follow steps that will give you peace of mind. With that being said, let's get into it.

LESSON #1: DRINK WATER, AND LOTS OF IT.

Drinking water is the most important of all lessons and a habit that we want to ingrain into our children's everyday routine. Water makes up approximately 60% of your body weight. According to H.H. Mitchell, *Journal of Biological Chemistry 158*, "The brain and heart are composed of **73%** water, and the lungs are about **83%** water."[1] Water is involved in every cellular activity in the body, and when you don't drink enough water, those processes are not as efficient. Some of those processes include metabolism, removing toxins from the body, bringing nutrients to your cells, enabling kidneys to filter properly, etc. Even mild dehydration can drain your energy, make you tired, cause overeating, constipation and prevent weight loss. Another interesting fact about the importance of proper water intake is that most cravings are due to dehydration, so if your child has a craving, first see if it subsides after drinking a glass of water before giving into it.

According to F. Batmanghelidj, M.D, "Dehydration causes disease, depression, stress, weight gain, etc. We can prevent many of these issues by drinking water on a regular basis."[2]

---

1 Batmanghelidj, F. Your Body's Many Cries for Water: You Are Not Sick, You Are Thirsty! Don't Treat Thirst with Medications. Falls Church, VA: Global Health Solutions, 1995. Print.

2 Batmanghelidj, F. Your Body's Many Cries for Water: You Are Not Sick, You Are Thirsty! Don't Treat Thirst with Medications. Falls Church, VA: Global Health Solutions, 1995. Print.

What exactly does drinking water on a regular basis mean, you ask? While it used to be "drink eight glasses of water per day," the one-size-fits-all rule, now we are seeing more information that suggests that the amount of water we drink should be more customized to individual needs. **A metric to help you gauge the proper amount of water intake is to drink ½ ounce to 1 ounce per pound of your body weight**[3]. So if you weigh 100 lbs., then you should be drinking between 50-100 ounces water per day. Be sure to remember that the level of activity, weather, etc. determines where you fit in that range. So if your kids are tired, sluggish and cranky, try giving them a glass of water.

It's never too early to get kids in the habit of drinking water so that it doesn't feel like a chore later on in life. When I limited my children's fluid intake of non-water beverages to 1 cup per day, their water intake increased. To facilitate this, I strategically put a glass of water near them as they do their homework, another glass by their bedside (only after they were toilet trained) and always have water in the car during any drive longer than 10 minutes. Having it always accessible and nearby helps solidify this habit.

It's important to remember that you are your kid's biggest and best role model. By drinking a lot of water yourself, your children are likely to want to mimic the habit. For a lot of us, the importance of drinking water wasn't something that was very highly stressed as we were growing up.

---

3 Batmanghelidj, M.D., F. "Frequently Asked Questions." WaterCure. N.p., n.d. Web. 19 Sept. 2015.

We're only now learning the importance of staying well-hydrated. A trick I use at work is to make sure I always have a glass by my desk. Whenever the glass is empty, I use that as a signal to get up, fill my cup, walk around and go to the bathroom from having drunk all that water. A good way to measure if you or your kids are drinking enough water is to check the color of urine. The darker the color, the more dehydrated you might be. Ideal color is pale yellow or clear. If it is dark yellow, drink up!

If making sure you're drinking enough water every day wasn't enough of a challenge, another thing to consider is the pH balance of the water you drink. According to Merriam-Webster dictionary, "pH is a number between 0 and 14 that indicates if a chemical is an acid or a base."[4] pH can either be alkaline or acidic. pH is measured on a scale of 1–14, with 1 being extremely acidic and 14 being highly alkaline. Water should be at least 7.4 pH, which is the same level as your blood or higher for optimum health and hydration. You are probably wondering *what does this all mean and why does it matter?*

Let me explain: **Our bodies work best when our body is alkaline**. If it is too acidic, it can cause inflammation, which is a breeding ground for ailments, disease and a variety of health issues. Imagine a fish tank. When a fish tank is clean, water is flowing through the filtration system, the water is clear and fish swim quickly to and fro. As the fish tank gets dirty, the water gets cloudy, algae starts to form on the

---

4 Merriam-Webster. Merriam-Webster, n.d. Web. 19 Sept. 2015.

surface and the fish don't move as quickly. Eventually, if the tank isn't cleaned, the fish will ultimately die.

I never realized that the water we drink can have different pH balance levels. This is not typically labeled on the water we drink, so how do we know? Well, you can use a simple and fun water experiment. My kids love putting their scientific hats on and testing different brands of water. I bought pH test drops for water pH. I found pH test drops for water pH with a color chart on Amazon for a pretty reasonable price (approximately $20.00). You need to get the drops, not the strips, to have an accurate reading of water pH, as the strips are used for testing the pH level of urine or saliva. My kids and I added a few drops of it into the different types of water we drank and waited to see which color the water turned. Light green, yellow and orange tinted water are progressively more acidic. Darker green, blue and purple tinted water are progressively more alkaline. I was shocked to see that the store brand water bottles I was sending my kids to school with every day had an acidity level of four!

Here I thought by replacing sugar-laden juice boxes with water bottles I was doing a good thing, only to discover that I was doing more harm than I realized. I added a filter to my faucet, and was thrilled to see that the tap water had an alkaline level of eight. So I went to Bed, Bath & Beyond to buy **BPA-free** water bottles (a must) and filled the bottles with filtered water from home and sent that with my kid's school lunch boxes. Doing this also saved a lot of money since I no longer had to buy a case of water every week, and reusing the same bottle was so much better for the environment. The Environmental Working Group (EWG), a non-profit organization whose mission is to protect human health and the environment, found 38 contaminants in 10 popular water bottle brands and recommends drinking filtered tap water as best option.[5]

Note: **BPA** *stands for bisphenol A, an industrial chemical used to make plastics and resins (lining of cans) since the 1960's. According to the Mayo Clinic there are "possible health effects associated with of BPA with respect to the brain, prostate glands and behavior of fetuses, infants and children."*[6] *While the FDA says BPA is safe in small doses, what is really a small dose over the course of someone's life and is that worth the risk? NO!*

---

5 "Most Bottled Water Brands Don't Disclose Information About Source, Purity and Contaminants." EWG. Environmental Working Group, 7 July 2009. Web. 19 Sept. 2015.

6 Zeratsky, Katherine, R.D., L.D. "Nutrition and Healthy Eating." What Is BPA? Should I Be Worried about It? Mayo Clinic, n.d. Web. 19 Sept. 2015.

pH Color Chart

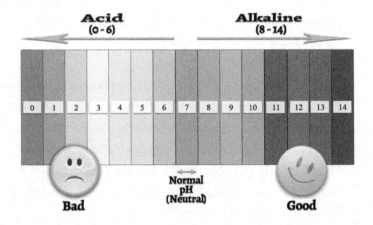

In the past, my kids had been used to drinking a lot of juice. I thought giving them a glass of OJ at breakfast every morning was part of a complete breakfast. **I later learned that unless juice is freshly squeezed, the pasteurization process kills all the nutrients, so what you are left with is a sugary beverage.**

Needless to say, it was tough in the beginning to wean them off. At first I tried to keep it to a minimum, watering down juice with water or seltzer. Instead of giving them a glass of OJ, I'd squeeze juice from one orange and give them the smaller portion it yields. Since lemon and lime become alkaline in your body despite the fact that they are acidic fruits, I started giving the kids my version of lemonade or limeade in the morning. I'd squeeze ¼ lemon or lime with 1 tablespoon of raw honey or 100% pure maple syrup into an eight-ounce glass of water to kick start their digestive system. Since the acidity of the lemon can erode tooth enamel long-term, I make sure my kids drink it with a straw. If you are giving this drink to your kids in the morning, make sure they brush their teeth before drinking or wait at least 60 minutes to brush after drinking[7]. The reason for this is that citric acid from lemons may soften enamel that is more prone to erosion by brushing.

This concoction was inspired by food activist, Vani Hari, aka "Food Babe." She says to kick start your system by drinking lemon water with cayenne pepper. Warning: Even though I drink it all the time now, the first few days of drinking the Food Babe's concoction can cause your lips to burn due to the cayenne. Thankfully, that sensation passes after a few days.

Now that we are all nice and hydrated, let's move on to learning how to read and interpret food labels to figure out what is really in our food.

---

7 "Don't Brush Teeth After Eating Acidic Foods - Bellevue Dentist." Bellevue Dental Care. N.p., 27 May 2015. Web. 19 Sept. 2015.

LESSON #2: ONE OF THE MOST VALUABLE THINGS YOU CAN TEACH YOUR KIDS IS HOW TO READ A FOOD LABEL.

Remember, there are 3 things to watch for when reading food labels:

1. Portion size.
2. The daily % intake of macronutrients, e.g., fat, protein, and carbohydrates on the food label.
3. The list of ingredients that make up the food, e.g., salt, oil, whole wheat flour.

In this lesson, we will understand portion sizes and daily % intake; in lesson #3, we will learn how to decipher the actual food ingredients.

Unfortunately, we can't take the marketing messages on products, such as "all natural" or "part of a healthy breakfast," at face value. The food industry is pressured to show continuous growth, profit and an increased market share to appease its investors. This is usually done by using ingredients that are cost effective and oftentimes intentionally addictive. These ingredients are not necessarily healthy ingredients, and they do not have the consumer's best interest at heart. Deciphering what you are eating can seem overwhelming at first, but once you get the hang of it, it can become second nature. I'll be sharing the tips/guidelines I've learned along the way to help you out.

The first step in learning about what we are eating is learning how to understand how to interpret the nutritional facts found on the label of these foods. Since preparing school snacks or lunches for our children is most easily done with pre-packed food, completely avoiding packaged food items is extremely difficult. **It's important for our kids to understand serving sizes as the first step towards understanding portion control.** I try not to eat dessert too often, but every once in a while I give in to my sweet tooth and splurge on my favorite dessert: ice cream. I bought a few pints of ice cream to share with my family. While it would have been so easy for my 11-year-old and me to scarf down a pint each on our own, I read the nutritional information and at first glance I thought, *Two hundred calories and 10 grams of fat; that's not a horrible splurge.* I then looked closer and realized that there were 4 servings in that little container. Knowing that we would have eaten 800 calories and 40 grams of fat was enough for my son and me to begrudgingly portion out a serving of it into a bowl and not step into the kitchen for the rest of the night. We're only human, and there's nothing wrong with a little indulgence every now and then. But it's important to remember that indulging in your cravings is, in the long run, so much less satisfying than indulging in taking care of your body. Nothing tastes as good as healthy feels.

Understanding Portion Size:

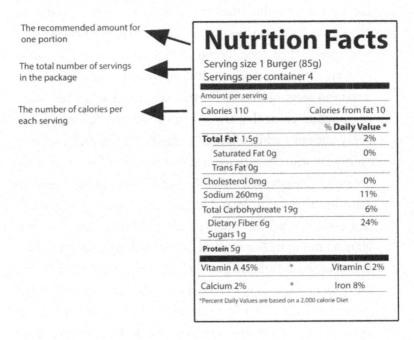

The recommended amount for one portion

The total number of servings in the package

The number of calories per each serving

Nutrition Facts

Serving size 1 Burger (85g)
Servings per container 4

Amount per serving

Calories 110		Calories from fat 10
		% **Daily Value** *
Total Fat 1.5g		2%
Saturated Fat 0g		0%
Trans Fat 0g		
Cholesterol 0mg		0%
Sodium 260mg		11%
Total Carbohydreate 19g		6%
Dietary Fiber 6g		24%
Sugars 1g		
Protein 5g		
Vitamin A 45%	*	Vitamin C 2%
Calcium 2%	*	Iron 8%

*Percent Daily Values are based on a 2,000 calorie Diet

When reading food labels, once we understand the amount of food as indicated by portion size, next is to understand the amount of macronutrients in the food as indicated by the % of daily value to get a clearer picture of what we are consuming. For example when I look at the number of calories, total fat, total carbohydrates, sodium and protein per serving, I am looking at % of daily value as a rough gauge as to the amount of daily value it represents.

Understanding Portion Size

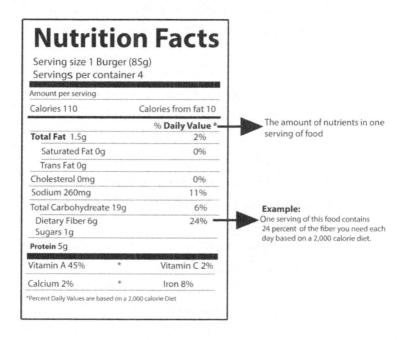

Nutrition Facts

Serving size 1 Burger (85g)
Servings per container 4

Amount per serving

Calories 110   Calories from fat 10

	% Daily Value *
Total Fat 1.5g	2%
Saturated Fat 0g	0%
Trans Fat 0g	
Cholesterol 0mg	0%
Sodium 260mg	11%
Total Carbohydrate 19g	6%
Dietary Fiber 6g	24%
Sugars 1g	
Protein 5g	

Vitamin A 45%	*	Vitamin C 2%
Calcium 2%	*	Iron 8%

*Percent Daily Values are based on a 2,000 calorie Diet

The amount of nutrients in one serving of food

Example:
One serving of this food contains 24 percent of the fiber you need each day based on a 2,000 calorie diet.

Note: All of the nutrients listed in the above-illustrated label are not meant to add up to 100%. Rather, each % nutrient listed reflects the amount consumed of a recommended 100% daily intake based on a 2,000 calorie diet. Also, if a food has 20% or more of a certain nutrient, it is a good source of that nutrient. In the example above, this food is a good source of fiber.

A few additional things to watch out for to help you make sense of the food label:

- **Total fat:** There are 4 types of fat a food may contain: saturated fat, trans fat, polyunsaturated fat and monounsaturated fat.
  - ○ *Trans fat* should be avoided at all costs.
  - ○ *Polyunsaturated and monounsaturated fats* are the healthy fats and are heart healthy.
  - ○ *Saturated fat* should be limited and eaten in moderation.
- **Total sodium:** The amount of salt contained in the food. It is recommended that we consume 1500-2000 milligrams per day.
- **Total carbohydrates:** I look for foods higher in dietary fiber and lower in sugar.
  - ○ *Dietary fiber:* Foods containing less than 2 grams of fiber don't really contain fiber. It is recommended to have at least 25 grams per day (based on a 2000 calorie diet per day) as fiber helps us digest food and keeps us full longer. Fiber can be found in whole grains, legumes, fruits and vegetables.

As it relates to total carbohydrates, I'll go into further depth as to how sugar is enemy #1 later in this book, but wanted to call attention to the fact that **sugar never has % daily value listed in the nutritional facts.** This is probably because most processed foods contain so much sugar that this transparency would surely reduce product sales. According to the American Heart Association, the average American consumes 52-80 grams of added sugar per day versus the recommended range of 12-36 grams daily.[8]

On the next page is a grid that lists calorie guidelines by age based on three levels of activity, according to the United States Department of Agriculture Center for nutrition policy. [9] While I've referred to this as a frame of reference, I understand that different people thrive better under different guidelines or parameters. While I personally believe that you don't need to count calories if you teach your kids to eat healthy foods and listen to their body's hunger and satiety cues, it never hurts to have the information readily available.

---

8 "Frequently Asked Questions about Sugar." Frequently Asked Questions about Sugar. American Heart Association, 19 May 2014. Web. 11 Oct. 2015. <http://www.heart.org/HEARTORG/GettingHealthy/Nutrition-Center/HealthyDietGoals/Frequently-Asked-Questions-About-Sugar_UCM_306725_Article.jsp>.

9 A. Estimated Calorie Needs per Day by Age, Gender, and Physical Activity Level. (n.d.): n. pag. United States Department of Agriculture. Web. 18 Sept. 2105.

ESTIMATED CALORIE GUIDELINES
(BY AGE, GENDER AND ACTIVITY LEVEL)

Gender	Age (years)	Sedentary	Moderately Active	Active
Child	2-3	1,000	1,000-1,400	1,000-1,400
Female	4-8	1,200	1,400-1,600	1,400-1,800
	9-13	1,400 -1600	1,600-2,000	1,800-2,200
	14-18	1,800	2,000	2,400
	19-30	2,000-1800	2,200 -2000	2,400
	31-50	1,800	2,000	2,200
	51+	1,600	1,800	2,000-2,200
Male	4-8	1.200-1,400	1,400-1,600	1,600-2,000
	9-13	1,600-2,000	1,800-2,200	2,000-2,600
	14-18	2,000-2,400	2,400-2,800	2,800-3,200
	19-30	2,600-2,400	2,800-2,600	3,000
	31-50	2,400-2,200	2,600-2,400	3,000-2,800
	51+	2,000	2,200-2,400	2,400-2,800

Now that we feel confident with how to read and what to look out for on a nutritional food label, we can move on to lesson #3, which deciphers what most people overlook: the actual ingredients listed on the food package.

LESSON #3: TEACH YOUR KIDS TO GO BEYOND THE NUTRITIONAL LABEL AND UNDERSTAND LISTED FOOD/INGREDIENTS.

Understanding the information on nutritional labels is only the first step, and it can be misleading without going beyond the label to reading the ingredients. There are 18 tips that I'd like to share with you as a sort of "cheat sheet" since none of us have time or energy to decipher what all these ingredients mean.

Warning: Once you teach your kids these rules, there is no turning back. My kids actually got a bit obsessed with reading food ingredient labels and would ask their friends if they could read labels in the lunches they brought. I then had the opposite challenge to explain to them that they can't judge the food their friends were eating and to find a balance of when to help educate friends on what they are learning and be a source of knowledge to them when they ask versus imposing beliefs on them, especially while they were eating.

TIP #1: ANYTHING YOU CAN'T PRONOUNCE IS PROBABLY NOT THAT GOOD FOR YOU.

Chances are if you can't pronounce it, it was created in a lab. We aren't meant to eat foods manipulated through science. When food is altered this way, it is considered to be processed food. Processed foods are "dead" food and don't have the same life energy as a whole food. I truly believe that we take on the energy of the food we eat. Do you want to get your life's energy from processed dead food or lively whole foods?

TIP #2: THE FEWER INGREDIENTS LISTED, THE BETTER.

All the best foods for you are real, single-ingredient foods. Think about it...all fruits, vegetables, nuts, seeds, oils, and eggs are single-ingredient foods. On the contrary, some of the more common packaged snack foods, such as Cheez-It® Snack Mix, for example, have over 100 ingredients. When I do buy packaged snack foods for my kids, I look for healthier alternatives. For example, in my opinion, potato chips should have three ingredients: potatoes, oil and salt.

TIP #3: PAY ATTENTION TO THE ORDER IN WHICH THE INGREDIENTS ARE LISTED.

The ingredients that make up the largest quantity are listed at the beginning of the list. If **sugar** is listed in the top three ingredients, there's probably a good chance that the nutritional content of that item is not great.

TIP #4 STAY AWAY FROM GENETICALLY MODIFIED ORGANISMS, A.K.A "GMOs."

GMOs are organisms whose genetic makeup (DNA) have been altered in a way that does not occur naturally. This is done by inserting a piece of DNA into different species creating a new life form. Mainly this process is designed to be inserted into crops, such as corn, soybeans and others, modifying these crops to survive herbicide treatment, produce their own pesticides, and resist certain diseases. There are several problems with altering the DNA of our food to become more resistant to pesticides. We are altering the DNA of food that is supposed to feed our cells. But nobody really knows how these Franken-foods react in our system on a cellular level.

Another problem is that it has been estimated that the United States uses 1.2 billion pounds of pesticides per year on crops, but only a mere .01% actually does what it is supposed to and reaches the bugs.[10] Meanwhile, there are a number of health risks from pesticides ranging from skin irritation, hormone disruption, birth defects, blood and nerve disorders, reproduction defects and cancer. Washing the crop isn't the solution either as at least one pesticide remains on 63% of commonly purchased produce even after it has been washed, according to a study conducted by the Environmental Working Group.

Proponents of GMOs will say that they are no different than non-GMO crops and that GMOs are feeding the world and ending world starvation. The sad truth is that quite the opposite is happening. Studies show time and time again that farmland use in connection with GMO-related

---

10 Donovan, Travis. "Pesticides In Food: What To Eat And What To Avoid (PHOTOS)." The Huffington Post. TheHuffingtonPost.com, 25 May 2011. Web. 11 Oct. 2015. <http://www.huffingtonpost.com/2010/05/20/pesticides-in-food-what-t_n_581937.html>.

crops shows a constant depletion of nutrients, and that using GMO crops literally "kills" the earth. Statistics also show that GMO crops are yielding fewer crops per acreage than non-GMO crops.

In short, we are the living guinea pigs of its effects, as these crops were not properly tested prior to being released into our food supply. Some of those ill effects include increased use of pesticides, reproductive issues, allergies, diseases, and have been linked to tumors in rats.

The main eight GMO crops are soy, corn, alfalfa, cotton, zucchini, papaya, sugar and canola. In North America, 70% of our packaged foods contain GMO ingredients. But since the FDA, due to enormous pressure from lobbyists, doesn't require labeling of GMO foods, most consumers have no idea what is in their food. Just to compare the USA to the rest of the world, 64 other countries label GMOs and at least 25 countries either restrict or ban them altogether.[11] How does that make you feel?

So how can you avoid eating GMOs? The foolproof way to do this is to eat organic. **Organic food cannot contain synthetic pesticides, antibiotics, or growth hormones. Animals labeled as organic have not been fed the GMO seed.**

---

11 "GMO Defined." GMO Awareness. GMO-Awareness.com, 29 Apr. 2011. Web. 12 Oct. 2015. <http://gmo-awareness.com/all-about-gmos/gmo-defined/>.

Each produce food label has a numbered code. This is very important since it will help you in identifying GMO products. Pay attention to the codes on the stickers of the fruits and veggies:

- **Five-digit codes** that start with **8** is a **GMO crop.**
- **Four-digit codes** that start with **3 or 4 are conventional crops.**
- **Five-digit codes** that start with **9 are the best option identifying the crops as organic.**

In the absence of requiring the labeling of GMOs, health-conscious companies can go through a process where once they are verified as GMO-free, they can add a **non-GMO Project Verified Seal** to their product. I look for that seal in processed foods I purchase. In today's smart phone era I also highly recommend you download the free app "Check GMO," which is available on both OS and Android platforms. This app will allow you to scan the UPC code of an item and the app will let you know if the scanned product contains GMO ingredients. The Institute for Responsible Technology is a non-profit organization whose mission is to educate policy makers and consumers on GMOs. They created a "non-GMO shopping guide" to help consumers make educated decisions about products during the shopping process.

Below is a list of ingredients that can be **hidden sources of GMOs** unless organic or specified otherwise. For a more exhaustive list, please refer to nongmoshoppingguide.com.

Ascorbic Acid	Maltodextrin
Aspartame	Soy Lecithin
Baking Powder	Soy Sauce
Colalmin (B12), B2 and Biotin	Tempeh
Beta Carotene	Textured vegetable protein
Cellulose	Tocopherols (vitamin E)
Sugar (unless specified as Cane)	Xanthan Gum
Fructose	Whey
Ingredient containing Soy E.g., soy lecithin, soy sauce	Ingredient containing Corn E.g., corn starch, corn meal

Note: In November 2015, the FDA approved genetically modified salmon despite concerns about its safety for human consumption or the environment. Another reason to only eat wild fish as it is not required to label GMO salmon as such.

TIP #5 AVOID MSG AND ITS HIDDEN FORMS.

Monosodium glutamate, more commonly known as MSG, is a flavor-enhancer added to many foods like Chinese food, canned foods, and processed meats. Its sole purpose is to make food taste better so that you crave more of it. Sneaky right? Little do we know just how badly our bodies can react to this flavor enhancer. I have a good friend that gets so violently ill from eating MSG that she can't order from a restaurant without asking if they use it. According to the Mayo Clinic, "Some of the reactions of MSG Symptom Complex are headache, flushing, sweating, facial pressure or tightness, numbness, tingling or burning in the face, neck and other areas, rapid, fluttering heartbeats, heart palpitations, chest pain, nausea, and weakness."[12]

Keep your eyes open to some hidden forms of MSG. If an ingredient contains any one or more of the following words, it most likely contains free glutamic acid, the main component of MSG: hydrolyzed, yeast extract, amino acids, and/or protein. Another tip is that if you see disodium 5'-guanylate (E 627), disodium 5'-inosinate (E-631), or disodium 5'-ribonucleotides (E 635) listed on the label, MSG is most likely in that product as well since those ingredients work in tandem with MSG to enhance flavor.

---

12 Zeratsky, Katherine, R.D., L.D. "Nutrition and Healthy Eating."Monosodium Glutamate (MSG): Is It Harmful? Mayo Clinic, n.d. Web. 23 Sept. 2015. <http://www.mayoclinic.org/healthy-lifestyle/nutrition-and-healthy-eating/expert-answers/monosodium-glutamate/faq-20058196>.

Note: For a good resource to view an extensive list of names of ingredients that contain processed free glutamic acid, check out the following website: http://www.truthinlabeling.org/hidden-sources.html

TIP #6 PRESERVATIVES ARE PRESERVING THE FOOD, NOT YOUR HEALTH.

This is another case of chemicals being put in our food for financial profits with no consideration of the consumer's best interest. Preservatives are added so that the product can stay on the shelf as long as possible without going bad. I don't know about you, but the thought of eating something that has been on the shelf for months or even years grosses me out. Not to mention the fact that preservatives are actually harmful to our health. They have been said to cause breathing problems, hyperactivity in kids, heart damage, and even cancer. According to the Mayo Clinic, "removing preservatives from your diet can reduce the symptoms and severity of asthma." Preservatives can be found in most processed foods as well. Foods like hot dogs, sodas, etc., are common breeding grounds for preservatives, yet again proving another reason why it is important to read ingredients in the foods we eat.

A cheat sheet list of preservatives:

- Aspartame
- Sodium Benzoate
- BHA (Butylated Hydroxyanisole)
- BHT (Butylated Hydroxytoluene)
- Nitrite, i.e., Sodium Nitrite
- Sulfites (Potassium Bisulfite, Potassium Metabisulfite, Sodium Sulfite & Sulfur Dioxide)
- Nisin
- Taurine
- Ascorbic Acid
- Citric Acid
- Benzoic Acid
- Sorbates (Sorbic Acid, Potassium Sorbate, Sodium Sorbate and Calcium Sorbate)

TIP #7 FOOD DYES/ARTIFICIAL COLORS ARE BAD, BAD, BAD.

Artificial colors are chemical dyes added to food and drinks. The purpose of including this additive in our food supply is usually to make the product look better for consumption in order to ultimately increase sales. According to WebMD, "Artificial food color is suspected of causing increased hyperactivity in children and the dye Yellow No. 5 has been thought to worsen asthma symptoms."[13] Our children are being exposed to these food dyes more and more,

---

13 Downs, Martin, MPH. "The Truth about 7 Common Food Additives."WebMD. WebMD, 17 Dec. 2008. Web. 19 Sept. 2015.

with the amount rising over 500% in the period between 1955 and 2010.[14] The American Academy of Pediatrics supports removing additives from the diets of children that struggle with ADHD. [15] These ingredients can be found in the weirdest places like pickles, so again, definitely, read the ingredients.

List of artificial colors to watch out for:
- FD&C Blue No. 1
- FD&C Blue No. 2
- FD&C Green No. 3
- FD&C Red No. 40
- FD&C Red No. 3
- FD&C Yellow No. 5
- FD&C Yellow No. 6
- Caramel Color

TIP #8 ARTIFICIAL FLAVORS, LIKE PERFUME FOR OUR TASTE BUDS, REALLY STINK.

Artificial flavors are flavors that are usually inedible and petroleum-based and synthesized in a lab for the purpose of either imitating or enhancing a natural flavor. Just

---

<http://www.webmd.com/diet/the-truth-about-seven-common-food-additives?page=1>.

14 "The Feingold Diet Program for ADHD." The Feingold Diet Program for ADHD. Feingold Association of the United States (FAUS), 2015. Web. 12 Oct. 2015. <http://www.feingold.org/>.

15 Schonwald, A. "ADHD and Food Additives Revisited." AAP Grand Rounds19.2 (2008): 17. Web.

like a lot of scents are mixed and matched to create the perfect fragrance, the same process is done by combining a lot of different tastes to find the "best" flavor. Best in this context does not mean healthy. Instead, it means the most flavorful and addicting so that consumers eat as much as possible and buy more. They are declared in ingredient lists as "artificial flavor" and should be avoided.

TIP #9 "NATURAL FLAVORS" MIGHT NOT BE SO NATURAL.

According to the "Environmental Working Group" who rates more than 80,000 foods: "Natural flavor finds its way into more than a fifth of that roster of 80,000 foods with only salt, water, and sugar mentioned more frequently on food labels."[16] I used to think natural flavors were a safe and even healthy ingredient. According to the Code of Federal Regulations, natural flavor "contains the flavoring constituents derived from a spice, fruit or fruit juice, vegetable or vegetable juice, edible yeast, herb, bark, bud, root, leaf or similar plant material, meat, seafood, poultry, eggs, dairy products or fermentation products thereof, whose significant function in food is flavoring rather than nutritional."[17] That all sounds pretty harmless, right? Wrong!

---

[16] Andrews, David. "EWG's Food Scores Just Took the Work out of Grocery Shopping for Me!" EWG's Food Scores. Environmental Working Group, n.d. Web. 19 Sept. 2015. <http://www.ewg.org/foodscores/content/natural-vs-artificial-flavors>.

17 "CFR - Code of Federal Regulations Title 21." CFR - Code of Federal Regulations Title 21. U.S. Food & Drug Administration, 21 Aug. 2015. Web. 19 Sept. 2015.

What you probably didn't know is that the origin of those "natural" flavors doesn't have to be disclosed. So, if you are a vegetarian, you could be eating a food that contains natural flavors derived from beef without having to label it as such. Or as the food activist, Vani Hari aka the Food Babe, enlightened us in one of her insightful investigations, a **beaver's anal gland** is approved by the FDA as a form of natural flavor.[18] I don't know about you, but when I read that blog, I was beside myself. I also recently learned that natural flavors could contain synthetic chemicals, with the exception of organic natural flavors. I try to avoid foods with natural flavors, which isn't always successful given that they are so prevalent. Buying my kids a lot of snacks from the organic aisle does help.

The "real" natural flavors that enhance your food and are healthy are herbs and spices. Sprinkling some cinnamon in your oatmeal, adding parsley and cilantro in soups, stews and rice, tossing in fresh basil in pasta, brewing tea with fresh mint leaves are just a few ways I've incorporated these real natural staples into my kitchen.

TIP #10 AVOID CARRAGEENAN.

Carrageenan is an additive widely used in the food industry to gel, thicken or stabilize the food it's being added to. According to *Cornucopia*, animal studies show that "food-

---

18 Hari, Vani. "FOOD BABE TV: Do You Eat Beaver Butt?" Food Babe. Food Babe, 09 Sept. 2013. Web. 27 Sept. 2015. <http://foodbabe.com/2013/09/09/food-babe-tv-do-you-eat-beaver-butt/#more-14529>.

grade carrageenan causes gastrointestinal inflammation and higher rates of intestinal lesions, ulcerations, and even malignant tumors."[19] This ingredient can be found in some non-dairy milk, like almond, soy, rice, coconut, and it can be found in dairy products. It can even be found in organic foods, so it's definitely important to read the ingredients. A good resource is the Cornucopia Institute website, www.cornucopia.org. It lists the name brands that contain carrageenan and lists alternate brands that don't contain carrageenan.

TIP #11 MAKE SURE MILK DOESN'T HAVE RECOMBINANT BOVINE GROWTH HORMONE RBGH.

A lot of conventional dairy products contain rBGH, which is a GMO hormone given to cows to make them unnaturally produce more milk. This benefits the farmer only. It makes the cow's sick, causing infection of the udder and mastitis. The milk ends up being contaminated by the pus from the infection as well as the antibiotics used to treat it. Dr. Samuel Epstein, chairman of the Cancer Prevention Coalition, warns that "rBGH milk is both chemically and nutritionally different than natural milk and that excess levels of IGF-1 can cause breast, colon, and prostatecancers."[20] Purchasing organic milk and dairy products is the best way to make sure you are not ingesting this dangerous hormone.

---

19 "Carrageenan." Cornucopia Institute (n.d.): n. pag. Mar. 2013. Web. 19 Sept. 2015.

20 Epstein, Samuel S., M.D. "What's in Your Milk? An Expose on the DANGERS of Genetically Engineered Milk." What's in Your Milk? An Expose on the

TIP #12 MAKE SURE THE POULTRY PACKAGE INDICATES
THAT ANTIBIOTICS HAVE NOT BEEN ADMINISTERED.

The conditions of farm-raised animals are so poor
that farmers preventively give animals antibiotics so that
they don't get sick and negatively affect sales. The problem is
that as much as 80% of our precious antibiotics are given to
these animals as a preventative measure to increase sales.
This is a very dangerous practice since the overuse of antibiotics make it less prone to work as a last defense in the future
when we really need them.

Think about it, kids are ingesting traces of antibiotics in farm-raised meat products for years and will eventually build resistance to them when they really need them. On
a more spiritual level, the thought of eating an animal that
went through such suffering is hard to swallow, both literally
and figuratively. I do believe in harmony and positive energy
in the world around us as a part of our journey, so eating an
animal whose energy has been filled with such pain and suffering cannot be too good for us. Once again, for those of us
who eat poultry, **organic** poultry is the best way to ensure
that you and your family are not ingesting antibiotics unnec-
essarily.

DANGERS of Genetically Engineered Milk. Organic Consumers Association, 3 Jan.
2007. Web. 19 Sept. 2015. <https://www.organicconsumers.org/news/whats-your-
milk-expose-dangers-genetically-engineered-milk>.

Note: **No hormones added** label. Do not get confused between hormones and antibiotics.

> *USDA website states "Hormones are not allowed in raising hogs or poultry." Therefore, the claim "no hormones added" cannot be used on the labels of pork or poultry unless it is followed by a statement that says "Federal regulations prohibit the use of hormones." if you encountered a product that states "no hormones added" on the label, it does not mean that no antibiotics are added since hormones are not allowed regardless.[21]*

Another important note: Don't be fooled by **free-range, free-roaming, or cage-free labels** on poultry/eggs. This is just a marketing scam to make you think these chickens have a great life roaming freely in green pastures. When in reality, even though they are not in a cage, "most still have their sensitive beaks cut off with a hot blade and are crammed together in filthy sheds. They never go outside, breathe fresh air, feel the sun on their backs, or do anything else that is natural or important to them."[22]

---

21 "Meat and Poultry Labeling Terms." Meat and Poultry Labeling Terms. United States Department of Agriculture, 10 Aug. 2015. Web. 19 Sept. 2015. <http://www.fsis.usda.gov/wps/portal/fsis/topics/food-safety-education/get-answers/food-safety-fact-sheets/food-labeling/meat-and-poultry-labeling-terms/meat-and-poultry-labeling-terms

22 "Animals Used for Free-Range and Organic Meat." PETA Animals Used for FreeRange and Organic Meat Comments. PETA, n.d. Web. 20 Sept. 2015. <http://www.peta.org/issues/animals-used-for-food/organic-free-range-meat/>.

TIP #13 BUY BEEF THAT HASN'T BEEN GIVEN HORMONES OR ANTIBIOTICS.

Conventionally raised cattle are given hormones to promote growth and weight gain in order to expedite the timespan between birth and slaughter. It typically takes 2-3 years, if this process were to occur naturally. With the addition of hormones, this time span is shortened to 12-18 months. According to the Montana State University Cooperative Extension, "on average, 1.85 nanograms of growth hormone are detected in hormone supplemented beef per 3 ounce serving, compared to 1.3 nanograms in non-hormone supplemented beef." While these seem like minute levels of growth hormone, it represents a 42% increase and enough to cause the European Union to ban imports of U.S. beef to protect human health.[23] The same point of view I outline when it comes to antibiotics and poultry applies to antibiotics and beef as well. **Organic and grass-fed beef is best.** I also try to eat meat in moderation, limiting it to 1-2 times a week if possible.

TIP #14 ARTIFICIAL SWEETENERS CAN BE TOXIC.

This tip was one of the toughest for me personally. I can say that I was totally addicted to Diet Coke and needed

---

23 Roizman, Tracey. "Do Hormones in the Food Supply Affect the Human Body?" Healthy Eating. SF Gate, n.d. Web. 01 Nov. 2015.
<http://healthyeating.sfgate.com/hormones-food-supply-affect-human-body-2194.html>.

to drink at least one can every day. A meal wouldn't be complete without the flavor and carbonation satisfaction I'd feel with my lunch and/or dinner. I drank diet drinks because I thought they were the perfect combination of sweet without the extra calories you'd ingest in regular sodas. I since learned that not only are they harmful to your health (some research points to promoting cancer), they don't even make you lose weight as they can make you more susceptible to overeating. They can trick your body into increasing blood sugar as if you were drinking authentic sugar, to the point of causing diabetes down the line.

Since consumers are becoming more aware that artificial sweeteners are not what they were cracked up to be, the industry started using more obscure names to hide these artificial sweeteners in their products. On the Dr. Oz website, there is an article setting forth a list of names for artificial sweeteners,[24] the top level of which I have summarized below.

Note: The only non-sugary sweetener that is supposed to be okay and actually alkaline in your body is stevia. But make sure it is **whole leaf stevia.**

24 "List of Names for Artificial Sweeteners." List of Names for Artificial Sweeteners. The Dr. Oz Show, 7 Mar. 2014. Web. 12 Oct. 2015. <http://www.doctoroz.com/article/list-names-artificial-sweeteners>.

List of artificial sweeteners to avoid:

- Acesulfame Potassium
- Aspartame
- Cyclamate
- Erythritol
- Glycerol
- Glycyrrhizin
- Hydrogenated Starch Hydrolysate (HSH)
- Isomalt
- Lactitol
- Maltitol
- Mannitol
- Neotame
- Polydextrose
- Saccharin
- Sorbitol
- Sucralose
- Tagatose
- Xylitol

TIP #15 ADDED SUGAR IS ENEMY #1.

There are two types of sugar: naturally occurring sugars in fruits (fructose) and milk (lactose) and added sugars that are added to foods. When I was growing up, fat was the enemy, which resulted in the market being flooded with a ton of low-fat and fat-free products. Since fat adds flavor, reducing or removing fat meant less flavor. Now who would want to buy that? Not me. So, in order to compensate for this loss in flavor, companies started to add sugar and salt.

Not only does sugar have zero nutritional value, it is horrible for our bodies. It is being accused of a slew of things, ranging from the more obvious diseases like diabetes, heart disease, and cancer, to the less obvious offenders like depression, decreased cognitive function, premature aging and more acne-prone skin. Added sugar that we don't burn off turns into fat by our liver. New research from Oregon State University and published in the journal of *Neuroscience* suggests that diets high in sugar and fat can alter our gut bacteria and as a result have a detrimental effect on what they refer to as "cognitive flexibility," which is the ability to adapt and adjust when the situation changes.[25] It is more addictive than cocaine, according to Dr. Mark Hyman, functional doctor and author of many books such as the "Blood Sugar Solution" and "The 10-day Detox Diet." So the more you eat

---

25 Sandle, Tim. "Excess Fat And Sugar Can Lead To Cognitive Decline - The Latest News." The Latest News. N.p., 24 June 2015. Web. 20 Sept. 2015. <http://www.thelatestnews.com/excess-fat-sugar-can-lead-cognitive-decline/>.

products with added sugar, the more your body craves, causing a vicious circle and contributing to the epidemic of obesity our country is now facing.

It's not things like adding a teaspoon of sugar to everyday foods like tea or oatmeal that are the issue. It's all the added sugar in our foods like soda, candy, cakes, cookies, pies, fruit drinks, desserts, yogurt and processed grains and in things that we wouldn't even think would contain sugar that is causing this epidemic. For example, I recently looked at the ingredients for a supposedly healthy brand of frozen food where their chicken pesto pasta dish had corn syrup and molasses—two types of sugar. Unless you were reading the ingredients and aware of it, you wouldn't ever assume that your child would be ingesting half of the daily recommended amount of sugar in this "healthy" dish. I also learned in the movie *Fed Up* that unlike all other items listed on a nutritional label, when it comes to listing the amount of sugar it doesn't say what percentage of the daily allowance that represents.

According to the American Heart Association, women should have no more than 6 teaspoons per day and men no more than 9 teaspoons, which equals 24-36 grams of sugar a day. **Four grams** of sugar are equal to **one teaspoon.** For most American women, this is no more than 100 calories per day and no more than 150 calories per day for men. According to Family Education, kids are consuming as much as **seven times** their recommended daily intake.[26] Kids under 8

---

26 Nall, Rachel. "Daily Sugar Recommendations for Kids." LIVESTRONG.COM. LIVESTRONG.COM, 23 Apr. 2015. Web. 20 Sept. 2015. <http://www.livestrong.com/article/458552-how-much-sugar-per-day-for-kids/>.

should not have more than 3 teaspoons or 12 grams. Preteens and teens can have about 5 to 8 teaspoons per day (20-32 grams of added sugar). To put that into perspective, the CDC reports that the average American consumes 13-20 teaspoons or 52-80 grams of added sugar per day instead of the recommended 6-9 teaspoons (24-36 grams) per day, every day.

To summarize:

Age	Recommended Grams/Tsp per day
Eight and under	12 grams (3 tsp)
Eight and above	20-32 (5-8 tsp)
Adult Women	24 (6 tsp)
Adult Men	36 (9 tsp)

So when you hear about the obesity epidemic in this country and all the health issues that go along with it, you now know why. **Sugar is enemy #1**. Plainly and simply put.

Note: Do not be fooled! Sugar has so many names that just looking for the word "sugar" will not really tell you if a product contains sugar.

According to the American Heart Association, names for **added sugars** on labels include:

- Corn sweetener
- Corn syrup
- Fruit juice concentrate
- High Fructose corn syrup
- Honey
- Invert sugar
- Malt sugar
- Molasses
- Raw sugar
- Sugar (brown, white, powdered)
- Sugar molecules ending in "ose" (dextrose, fructose, glucose, lactose, maltose, sucrose)

The sugars I use in moderation:

- Organic sugar in the raw so that I at least know that sugar is not GMO
- Brown rice syrup
- Organic molasses
- Organic maple syrup
- Organic coconut palm sugar (for baking)
- Manuka honey
- Raw honey

I went on a 10-day sugar detox where I cut all sugar out of my diet with the only sugar content coming from berries. The first few days were very difficult, but by the end I got used to the taste of my morning tea without sugar, cut out my afternoon sugary beverage, etc. I felt great. I had a ton of energy and didn't have the drastic spikes and dips of energy. While it is difficult to eliminate sugar entirely and subject your kids to that almost impossible task, and live on this planet in a social way, I recommend taking steps to at least reduce their sugar intake without sacrificing too much.

One way to tackle reducing sugar intake is to take inventory of what your kids are drinking and reduce/cut the amount of sugar in those beverages. The obvious offenders are soda, energy, sports and fruit drinks that make up almost half of the added sugar consumed[27]. My kids were so used to drinking a glass of OJ every morning, juice box with their lunch, more juice with their afternoon snack and even more juice at dinner. I thought I was doing ok by not giving them any soda products or the obvious sugar/water drinks you find in drinks like Capri Sun®, Kool-Aid®, Sunny D®, Hi-C®, etc.

It was a long slow process (similar to the nicotine patch), but after few months, I was able to cut that to 1 cup of juice per day and even found creative ways to prolong that 1 cup by watering it down with seltzer or water. Also, in order for my kids to get the most nutrients from the juice, I try to fresh squeeze 1 fruit even if the portion yields less than 1 cup vs. buying the pasteurized store-bought version where a lot of the nutrients are killed with the heat in the pasteurization process. If you are thinking, *"I barely have time to get my kids*

---

27 WESTBROOK, JULIA. "19 Ways to Give Up Sugar." Rodale's Organic Life. Rodale's Organic Life, 11 Sept. 2015. Web. 20 Sept. 2015. <http://www.rodalesorganiclife.com/wellbeing/19-ways-give-sugar?cid=Soc_Facebook_RealSimple_0915&xid=soc_socialflow_facebook_realsimple>.

out of the house on time in the mornings; there is no way I'm freshly squeezing juice in the morning." I hear you. But there are ways to compromise. I don't do it every day, and I taught my kids how to manually squeeze fruit. They have fun doing it, and they can squeeze their own orange juice when they're in the mood for it.

Learning how to read a food label and the ingredients list is crucial in understanding the amount of sugar being added to store-purchased foods. Products that you should always be on the lookout for are yogurts, cereal, and flavored oatmeal. These can be deceptively high in sugar. When looking at a product's ingredient list, if sugar, syrup or anything ending in "ose" is listed among the first three ingredients, you can bet that the product is laden with sugar.

The best way to control the amount of sugar in food is through home-cooking. I've found that menu-planning for the week on Sundays, and even doing some of the prep work, made it easier during the week to eat healthy. To make things even more manageable, when you lock on a handful of recipes that your family enjoys, schedule those out during the week in a predictable fashion. Take, for example, my family's weekly menu: Every Monday is whole wheat or quinoa pasta with veggies, every Tuesday is stir fry tofu and brown rice, and every Wednesday is chicken, and so on, so that both your shopping list and prep can be easier to manage. Variety can come into play with the side dishes and on weekends when the family splurges by eating a few meals out.

TIP #16: TRANS FATS ARE DETRIMENTAL TO OUR HEALTH.

Trans fats are toxic to our bodies promoting heart disease and should be avoided at all costs. Trans fats are created when hydrogen is added to vegetable oil. They are added to food to preserve its quality, increase its flavor and make foods like baked goods feel soft and fresh. **In order to avoid them, stay away from any foods containing "partially hydrogenated oils" as declared in the food ingredients' list.**

Some well-known food items where trans fats can be hiding, are crackers, cookies, baked goods, margarine, microwave popcorn, coffee creamers, frosting and refrigerated dough products. Sometimes a label will say "0 grams trans fat" but it can still contain this toxic oil if the food contains less than 0.5 grams of trans fat per serving. This is a perfect example of how we need to make sure to go beyond the nutritional label and read the ingredients list since trans fats can be harmful even in small amounts. And let's be real, who eats only one serving size of cookies or popcorn? They can be found in a lot of processed foods, frozen foods and a lot of fast food chains with the exception of California and New York where the use of trans fats have been banned in restaurants. Trans fat increases the risk of type 2 diabetes and heart attack, even in small amounts. According to Vani Hari aka the Food Babe, "A 40-calorie-per-day increase in trans fat intake can lead to a 23% higher risk of heart disease. 40 calories is a mere 2% of a typical 2000 calorie per day diet.[28] So it's not hard to see how bad this really is. The good news is that partially hydrogenated oil is no longer considered safe by the FDA and food manufacturers have to phase it out by 2018. With all trans fats having to be removed from food items by 2018, we have one less battle to fight for our children's health.

TIP #17: TEACH YOUR KIDS ABOUT "DIRTY DOZEN" AND THE "CLEAN 15" TO SAVE THEM MONEY WHEN THEY START GOING GROCERY SHOPPING.

While organic is best, it does cost more than conventional produce. For those of us (myself included) that are on a budget, use the following method to help you identify which fruits and vegetables must be organic and which do not have to be, based on the amount of harmful pesticide use. The terms "Clean 15" and "Dirty Dozen" were coined by the Environmental Working Group (EWG), a non-profit, nonpartisan organization dedicated to protecting human health and the environment. [29]

28 Hari, Vani. "Food Babe Investigates - Chipotle Ingredients Now Available." Food Babe. N.p., 24 Mar. 2013. Web. 21 Sept. 2015. <http://food-babe.com/2013/03/24/a-food-babe-investigates-win-chipotle-posts-ingredients/>.

29 "EWG's Shopper's Guide to Pesticides in Produce™." EWG's 2015 Shopper's Guide to Pesticides in Produce™. Environmental Working Group, n.d. Web. 20 Sept. 2015. <http://www.ewg.org/food-news/?gclid=CjwKEAjwsvmvBRCT5ozKdmY7D4SJACyIoJmo7pix3C3aY4gbxz-tH4HOKswUa2ZzoRBHorytAWY-hoC1Bjw_wcB>.

On the next couple of pages are the two lists of produce:

Note: These lists get reviewed yearly so make sure to go to ewg.org for any future updates.

Clean 15 list:

Items below can be non-organic when purchasing.

1. Avocados
2. Sweet Corn
3. Pineapples
4. Cabbage
5. Sweet peas (frozen)
6. Onions
7. Asparagus
8. Mangos
9. Papayas
10. Kiwi
11. Eggplant
12. Grapefruit
13. Cantaloupe
14. Cauliflower
15. Sweet potatoes

Dirty Dozen list:

Purchase these items organic to avoid heavy pesticide use.

1. Apples
2. Cherry tomatoes
3. Cucumbers
4. Celery
5. Grapes
6. Nectarines
7. Peaches
8. Potatoes
9. Snap Peas
10. Spinach
11. Strawberries
12. Sweet Bell Peppers

Plus Hot pepper / Kale & Collard greens

Note: The dirty dozen produce has to be organic in order to avoid eating produce containing the highest pesticide load. The clean fifteen does not have to be organic due to having the lowest pesticide load.

I recently read an article about a Swedish study where the Swedish Environmental Research Institute (IVL) was commissioned by Coop, Sweden's largest grocery store cooperative to find out if switching to an all organic diet could reduce levels of pesticides found in our bodies.[30] They found a family that hadn't eaten organic foods previously and tested their pesticide load after a week of eating a conventional diet. They then ate only organic foods for two weeks and took blood tests again. The difference in pesticide levels before and after was significant, especially in the kids. On average, the pesticide loads in the bodies of the family members dropped by a factor of 9.5. The family also reported feeling better and vowed to change to an organic diet after the study was over.

Tip #18: Limit processed foods.

The most foolproof way to make sure you are following most of the above tips is by **limiting processed foods as much as possible**. And the processed foods you do buy for your family should be purchased while taking all of the above-mentioned tips into account.

When purchasing processed food products, **look for health conscious brands with a simple list of understandable ingredients**. For example, my kids love tortilla chips and before I became aware of these tips, I'd only look for chips that were lower in fat/calories than other brands. Now I look

---

30 Lemeric, Wendy. "Swedish Family Participating In Study Eats Organic Food For Two Weeks [WATCH VIDEO]." International Business Times AU. N.p., 13 May 2015. Web. 20 Sept. 2015. <http://www.ibtimes.com.au/swedish-family-participating-study-eats-organic-food-two-weeks-watch-video-1447895>.

for a brand where I can understand the ingredients, where the list of ingredients is short and doesn't include trans fat or GMO ingredients. I used to buy regular Tostitos® brand. I thought I was making a healthy choice for my family. A closer look at Tostitos® shows WHOLE GRAIN CORN, VEGETA-BLE OIL, SALT, and CALCIUM HYDROXIDE as the listed ingredients. I came to understand that the corn and oil ingredients are most likely GMO, and adding calcium hydroxide sounded suspect. I now buy the Simply Tostitos® brand that only has 3 ingredients and no GMO ingredients. It contains corn, salt and oil, which is all you need if you want to make tortilla chips at home.

Some of the snack brands I trust are:

Late July®	Skinny Pop®	Lundberg Farms®	Cascadian Farm®
Trader Joe's® Organic	Kettle Brand®	Eden® Organic	Annie's®
Mary's Gone Sticks & Twig Pretzels®	Whole Foods® Organic	Angies ® Boom Chicka Pop	EnviroKidz®
Go Raw® Cookies	Kind®	Colbee®	Way Better® Snacks

A great website that prides itself for selling healthy products at discounted prices is Thrive Market. This is a membership-based company, like Costco. I shop at Thrive

Market for a lot of my kids' school snacks since I found their prices to be better than retail stores. Plus they donate a free membership to someone in need for every membership purchased. To save $25 off your first order, sign up at HTTP://THRV.ME/CB8VHW. Again, don't forget to read the ingredients from even the more trustworthy brands. **In the end, the only person you can really trust is YOU!**

Another snack my kids were OBSESSED with was Cheez-It® Snack Mix. Again, I thought I was doing ok by buying it since it was baked. It also didn't have a lot of calories/fat for the portion size: 140 calories and 4.5 grams fat per ½ cup serving. But when I became knowledgeable about looking beyond the nutritional label and reading the ingredients, I was shocked about what I was feeding my kids all these years. The absurd number of ingredients in this product was over 100. So many of the ingredients are difficult to pronounce, like disodium phosphate, disodium inosinate, maltodextrin, etc. Some of the more toxic ingredients include MSG, GMO corn, soy, and canola, food additives, like maltodextrin, and added forms of sugar in the form of corn syrup, molasses and sugar. The dairy products in here most likely came from cows that were given synthetic hormones and antibiotics. If you can't pronounce a lot of the ingredients and there are too many ingredients listed, then walk away.

A better substitute for Cheez-It® brand is Annie's® Organic Cheddar Snack Mix. While it has similar calorie/fat to Cheez-It®, the ingredients are light years better. They use organic ingredients, which means it cannot contain MSG, dairy with hormones/antibiotics, or anything artificial. Of course, any of these processed snacks is not as good as fruits and vegetables, so one way to balance things out is to give a snack combo of fresh and packaged snacks. A few examples of these combo's are snack mix with a fruit, or crunchy veggies like carrots or celery, with a dip like peanut butter or hummus.

Note: Another tip I learned along the way is that if a product's label lists vitamins— for example, Cheez-It® contain Vitamin B1, Vitamin B2, and Folic Acid—it is because the actual ingredients in the product itself are devoid of nutrients.

To summarize, below is list of all of the 18 tips at a glance:

Tip #1 *Anything you can't pronounce is probably not that good for you.*

Tip #2 *The fewer ingredients listed the better.*

Tip #3 *Pay attention to the order in which the ingredients are listed.*

Tip #4 *Stay away from GMOs (or genetically modified organisms).*

Tip #5 *Avoid MSG, and its hidden forms.*

Tip #6 *Preservatives are preserving the food, not your health*

Tip #7 *Food dyes/Artificial colors are bad, bad, bad.*

Tip #8 *Artificial flavors, like perfume for our tastebuds, really stink.*

Tip #9 *Natural flavors might not be so natural.*

Tip #10 *Avoid Carrageenan.*

Tip #11 *Make sure milk doesn't have Recombinant Bovine Growth hormone (rBGH).*

Tip #12 *Make sure poultry package indicates that antibiotics have not been administered.*

Tip #13 *Buy beef that hasn't been given hormones or antibiotics.*

Tip #14 *Artificial sweeteners can be toxic and cause weight gain.*

Tip #15 *Added Sugar is enemy #1.*

Tip #16 *Trans fats are detrimental to our health.*

Tip #17 *Teach your kids about "Dirty Dozen" and "Clean 15" to save them money when they start going grocery shopping.*

Tip #18 *Limit processed foods.*

My hope is that this lesson left you with sufficient information for you to know what to watch out for when purchasing food for your family in order to ensure their health and longevity. I've been told by many mommy-friends of mine that nutrition isn't their strong suit and whenever they try to teach themselves about it, they get overwhelmed by how much information is out there. My hope is that this book does a good job of simplifying, consolidating and explaining in a very accessible way the information needed so that instead of feeling overwhelmed, you actually look forward to trying to apply it to your own lifestyle.

Now that you have the "don'ts" under your belt, let's talk about the "do's" and what you and your family should be eating in lesson #4.

LESSON #4 TEACH YOUR KIDS HEALTHY EATING HABITS FROM AN EARLY AGE.

For those of you who have picky eaters at home, I feel for you. I had the best of intentions to feed my kids healthy from the "get go." When they refuse to eat anything and you are worried they are not eating enough, it is really hard not to cave in and give them what they want to eat, even if you know it's not the healthiest of choices. Until I had kids, I had no idea there are actually two types of "picky eaters", and I am fortunate (wink, wink) to have one of each. My older son, Natanel, is picky in the sense that he is literally a food snob. He hates leftovers, can taste almost all the ingredients in any food, and has some texture issues on top of that. My younger son, Itai, is picky in the traditional sense. He likes "kid" food. Only recently did he start eating some veggies. There's only a handful of things he likes to eat but gets tired of his limited choices very quickly, making it extra challenging at meal time. In order to get their palettes used to healthier food, I try to sneak in healthy ingredients, where possible.

A few things I've done to hide healthy foods without my kids ever suspecting is to blend green veggies into pasta sauce, to mix in blended cauliflower into macaroni and cheese, to add protein powder and veggies to smoothies, etc. I also make the healthier versions of typical kid food. For example, baked vs. fried chicken nuggets, to help transition them to healthier eating. I have supplied bonus recipes in the appendix that have worked great in my family.

In addition to hiding healthy ingredients in foods kids like to eat, and modifying recipes into their healthier doppelganger, I also follow a principle I learned at the school of Integrative Nutrition called "crowding out". This is based on focusing on adding the good healthy stuff into your diet instead of focusing on taking away the bad unhealthy stuff from your diet. And by focusing on the positive and adding more healthy food, it will naturally "crowd out" the bad stuff since there simply won't be enough room for both. Let me illustrate this principle by telling you a story about my younger son's "white diet." This white diet consisted of pizza, pasta, potatoes and dairy products. He had bad eczema covering his arms and legs, and I had to take him to the emergency room twice within a six-month period for severe constipation. It became clear that his diet, lacking in fruits, vegetables and fiber was catching up to his little body. Instead of restricting him from all his current staples and making him feel deprived and resist, I let him eat his usual foods but incorporated more and more healthy options. As a result, the number of unhealthy options naturally decreased while the healthier options naturally increased.

With that being said, in this section, I will go into detail about the foods that promote good health and well-being—foods that fuel your cells, as well as your mind and spirit. At the end of this section, I included a General Nutrition Requirements table from the Build Healthy Kids website that I found to be a useful reference in listing approximate serving sizes by age. Again, this is just a reference. I don't measure or weigh my kid's food and believe that if they are eating healthy and listening to their bodies, they will intuitively know the right portion for them.

VEGGIES, THE MORE THE MERRIER.

Nobody has ever gone on an eating binge and eaten 10 bunches of broccoli or three bags of carrots like you would do with a bag of chips or a pint of ice cream. This is because these are foods from the earth that are made to nourish our body and souls. On page 68, there is a table that lists serving sizes by age. Knowing how hard it is to keep track of how many servings your child has eaten on a given day, I try to offer vegetables as a part of every meal and snack. At breakfast, I have some cut up tomatoes, cucumbers or avocado with a sprinkle of sea salt. I have a platter of cut up veggies (either cooked or raw depending on preference) like carrots, celery, mushrooms, or broccoli waiting for them when they get home from school. The trick is to offer it up to kids when they are hungry which makes them more likely to eat fruits and veggies, or at least try it. Also serving it up with some healthy dips like hummus, nut butter (e.g., almond butter that you can find in most grocery stores or on Amazon) or yogurt-based dip makes them more prone to eat it. In the appendix, I include a recipe in the snacks section on page 135 for a yogurt-based dip that my kids love.

For dinner, I try to have half the plate filled with some veggie, ¼ grain, and ¼ protein. This can be tough to accomplish, especially with those picky eaters, so getting creative on how to add nature's candy into our children's diet is well worth it. Before my kids were eating veggies more regularly, I served it with some butter, melted cheese or sprinkled with parmesan so that they could start to acquire the taste for the vegetable in question. Now some might say this is laden with fat and contradicts the point, but I'd still rather they have them eat vegetables this way than not at all. Later on as they grow up and eat vegetables more often, you can prepare them differently.

Another way to include veggies is to make a smoothie as an after school snack. Kids usually can't detect the taste of a handful of spinach leaves when mixed with fruits and other smoothie ingredients. In the appendix, you can take a look at some of the recipes that got my kids to eat more veggies, including a broccoli recipe that my older son created that, as a result, now causes him to eat broccoli several times a week.

FRUITS ARE NATURE'S CANDY.

The recommended daily allowance for fruits is between 1-2 cups a day depending on your child's age, gender and activity level. On page 68, there is a table that lists serving size by age. This is easier to accomplish than veggies, at least for my kids. I try to make fruits a part of every meal in their day. At breakfast I have some cut up fruit as a side or in cereal, yogurt or oatmeal. For lunch, I pack a sliced apple, orange, grapes or banana. And I offer it as dessert after dinner even if I have to throw in some whipped cream. Another way to include fruits is to make them a smoothie for an after-school snack. In the appendix, I include a few smoothie recipes that have become family staples, making it easier to get them to eat more fruits.

EAT THE COLORS OF THE RAINBOW.

Eight out of ten Americans don't have enough color in their diet. To try to teach kids from a young age to eat more fruits and vegetables, encourage them to eat the colors of the rainbow. And that doesn't mean Sour Patch™ kids, rainbow Goldfish® or Fruity Pebbles™. If you Google the "Eating by color chart," there are a lot of images outlining what fruits/veggies fit under the different colors and the various benefits for eating those colors. For example, getting enough yellow/orange into your diet (orange, carrots, banana, papaya, pineapple, yam, lemon, peach, etc.) is good for eye health, healthy immune system and healthy growth and development. Getting enough red into your diet (tomato, grapefruit, raspberries, watermelon, etc.) protects against cancer, heart disease, and overall DNA health.[31] It is recommended that we try to eat two foods from each color group daily.

My stance on fresh, frozen or canned produce is that eating fruits and vegetables in any shape or form is better than not eating any at all. That said, fresh is usually best, followed by frozen, and then canned. Canned vegetables usually contain an industrial chemical called BPA which can

---

31 Grussi, Rachel. "| GaiamTV." Gaiam TV. N.p., 3 Mar. 2014. Web. 12 Oct. 2015. <http://www.gaiamtv.com/article/5-colors-phytonutrients-eat-rainbow>.

seep into the food and can become harmful to our health in large doses. Frozen fruits and vegetables, at times, can be more nutritious than fresh if you are comparing freezing produce that is in season versus eating fresh produce that is not in season.

Eat whole grains for a great source of energy.

Children need between 2-7 ounces of grains per day, depending on age, gender and activity level. On page 68, there is a table that lists serving sizes by age. Whole grain is better than refined grain since there are a lot of vitamins and added fibers in the bran and germ layer. The same rationale applies to brown vs. white rice. As a general rule of thumb, brown grain products are whole grains while white grains have been bleached and processed. I love making quinoa since it also has a lot of protein. I've also experimented with a few lesser known grains like millet, buckwheat, farro and bulgur. I've had more luck with kids eating or even tasting these foreign foods if they helped me make them. At least in my house, it's not as hard to get them to eat grains. My challenge is to get them to replace more of the refined grains like organic white bread with organic whole grain or replace white rice with brown rice or quinoa. A lot of processed foods tout whole-grain on their packaging. How do you know if this is true or just false marketing? A great clue that I learned from Dr. David L. Katz of the Yale School of Medicine and nationally-renowned nutrition expert is to look at fiber content on the nutritional label. If it is 1 gram or less, it is not a whole grain but a "whole grain imposter."[32] In the appendix, there are a couple healthy grain recipes that include veggies too.

HEALTHY PROTEIN IS THE BUILDING BLOCKS TO HEALTHY BODY AND MIND

The recommended serving of protein for kids is between 2-6 ounces a day depending on age, gender and activity level. Healthy examples of protein are chicken, lean beef, turkey, pork, tofu, tempeh, fish, beans and eggs. When purchasing tofu, look for organic and fermented to ensure it doesn't contain GMO soy. Fish should always be wild as farmed raised fish is given a lot of antibiotics which we ingest when we eat it.

A few days a week I feed my family organic eggs for breakfast. Since my younger son went through a stage where he loved egg salad and now wants nothing to do with it or any other egg product, he usually doesn't eat protein in the morning. For lunch, they occasionally have a sandwich, salad or wrap, with protein as its base. Dinner is when they get their primary source of protein. The easiest way to cook protein like chicken is to season it with spices of your choice, add some olive oil, salt, and pepper and bake it in the oven. A fun and easy way to prepare fish is to put seasonings, herbs, lemon juice and olive oil wrapped like a tent in aluminum foil

32 Katz, David, and Catherine Katz. "Nutrition Detectives." A Katz & Katz Production Family Edition (2009): n. pag. Katz & Katz Production, 31 Mar. 2009. Web. 18 Sept. 2015. <http://www.turnthetidefoundation.org/NDmaterials/ND_Family_edition.pdf>.

and bake it. Cooking in this aluminum foil pocket makes fish flaky and delicious. On Monday's I try to go meatless to minimize animal protein by making either beans, tofu or fish. Go to the appendix for some creative ways to prepare healthy proteins–including a recipe for nut-crusted fish, the only fish dish my kids actually crave.

FAT DOES NOT MAKE YOU FAT.

That's right, I'll say it again: Fat does not make you fat. It is excess carbs and sugar that contribute to unwanted weight gain. Fat helps with the absorption of nutrients, keeps you full and adds flavor to food. Fat from oils provides essential fatty acids necessary for adequate growth and development. Don't be scared to feed your family healthy fats.

A few examples of healthy fats:
- Nuts (e.g., almonds, walnuts, pistachios, Brazil nuts, etc.)
- Seeds (e.g., sunflower, chia, flax, etc.)
- Avocado
- Cold-pressed organic oils (e.g., olive, coconut, and avocado)

DAIRY IS NOT THE ONLY FORM OF CALCIUM

Did you know that humans are the only species that drink another animal's milk after weaning? How the body reacts to dairy varies greatly from person to person. There are some who can't tolerate it. They have all sorts of issues where intolerance to milk shows up in digestive issues, eczema, etc. If you suspect your kid has digestive issues, you may want to try eliminating dairy for a while and see if that makes an impact. I try to limit dairy in my house since my younger son has eczema. Since he loves his cereal in the morning, I try to mix ½ dairy and ½ nut milk to minimize dairy. Since it is very important that children get the calcium needed for strong bones and teeth, getting creative with making sure they get their needed calcium is important. Leafy greens, seafood, legumes, and fruit also contain calcium and many foods and drinks like orange juice are fortified with calcium. Some foods that my kids enjoy are oranges, almonds, canned salmon (made like tuna salad) and tofu.

Again I wanted to mention that I follow the 80/20 rule when it comes to adhering to my own advice. I try to stick to it Monday through Friday and splurge more on weekends when we tend to eat out. In order to sustain this healthy lifestyle long-term, it is important to have balance and still live and enjoy what our society has to offer. To have my kids participate in their friends' birthday parties eating pizza and cake, and for me to go out once in a while on a date night or girls' night out and splurge without thinking about ramifications. This 80/20 guideline is what allows me and my kids to feel satiated and happy to start anew Monday morning drinking green juice, eating those fruits and vegetables, and trying new healthy foods.

General Nutrition Requirements
By BuildHealthykids.com[33]
(Based on moderate level of activity, 30 min or less daily)

Food Group	Kids 2-3	Kids 4-8	Boys 9-13	Boys 14-18	Girls 9-13	Girls 14-18
Calories	1000	1200-1400	1800	2200	1600	1800
Total Grains	3 Ounces	4-5 ounces	6 ounces	7 ounces	5 ounces	6 ounces
Vegetables	1 cup	1½ cups	2½ cups	3 cups	2 cups	2½ cups
Fruits	1 cup	1½ cups	1½ cups	2 cups	1½ cups	1½ cups
Milk	2 cups	2 cups	3 cups	3 cups	3 cups	3 cups
Meat/Beans	2 ounces	3-4 ounces	5 ounces	6 ounces	5 ounces	5 ounce
Oils	3 tsp.	4 tsp.	5 tsp.	6 tsp.	5 tsp.	5 tsp.
Discretionary (in calories)	165	170	195	290	130	195

33 "Build Healthy Kids | Nutrition 101 | The Basics Made Simple." Build Healthy Kids | Nutrition 101 | The Basics Made Simple. N.p., n.d. Web. 27 Sept. 2015. <http://www.buildhealthykids.com/genrequirements.html>.

Now that we are armed with the knowledge of the do's and don'ts of healthy eating, let's turn to another key component—nourishing and rejuvenating our body through exercise.

LESSON #5: EXERCISE: GET YOUR KIDS INVOLVED IN PHYSICAL ACTIVITY EARLY ON.

Now that we went into great lengths talking about food, let's take a look at another important part of maintaining a healthy body—and that is exercise! There are many benefits of exercise for both your body and mind. Regular physical activity can help you fall asleep faster, deepen your sleep, improve your mood, and boost your energy. It can relieve stress, ease depression and anxiety, and improve your memory. Exercise releases endorphins in the brain and helps relax the muscles and relieve tension in the body. Since the body and mind are so closely linked, when your body feels better so does your mind. Finally, regular physical activity can help control weight and help prevent or manage a wide range of health problems and concerns. According to the Mayo Clinic, you should aim for at least 30 minutes of physical activity every day as a general rule of thumb.[34]

Despite all these amazing benefits, incorporating regular physical activity into your life is very tough unless

---

34 Laskowski, Edward R., M.D. "Fitness." Exercise: How Much Do I Need Every Day? Mayo Clinic, 3 Jan. 2014. Web. 01 Nov. 2015. <http://www.mayo-clinic.org/healthy-lifestyle/fitness/expert-answers/exercise/faq-20057916>.

you've made physical activity a habit. That is why it is important to introduce exercise and staying active as a habit early on in your child's life so that it is part of his or her lifestyle and not something that is perceived as optional as they grow into adulthood. The toughest part about introducing a fitness program of any sort into your life is making it a habit, so the sooner you can do this in your child's life the better. I personally didn't have exercise as part of my early childhood. Sports were perceived as more of a boy's thing to do. It wasn't until middle school that I tried dance class, and then in high school I joined a gym to lose weight. It wasn't uncommon for me to go through spurts of working-out regularly followed by many months of inactivity. I usually started working-out a lot up front and then within a couple weeks, I would get physically sick and stop working out to recuperate from my illness. Then when I was better I wouldn't go back to working out. I perceived it as a chore but after I did it, I was glad that I did. But it took all my willpower to muster the energy and motivation to do it. It is just in the last couple years that I've consistently exercised and actually looked forward to it. I accomplished this by finding a type of exercise I enjoyed like Pilates, or enlisting a buddy to motivate me to take classes that ordinarily would be more difficult for me to motivate myself on my own. That buddy was my husband. I started taking a spin class every Sunday with my husband where we motivated each other to enjoy having that shared activity in common.

I've found it important to expose kids to many different types of sports to help them figure out what they like since they are more likely to incorporate it into their life if they enjoy it. Every kid is different and should have the space to figure out what they enjoy and where they can excel. My older son has no interest in ball-type sports but excels in swimming. While my younger son wants nothing to do with the pool and is obsessed with soccer and hockey.

Another way to exercise is through charitable walks and races. This approach really adds a lot of "bang for your buck"—it promotes physical activity, quality family time and teaches about charitable causes and giving. This can be a fun activity to do with friends, making it a fun social activity as well. Websites like www.thewalkingsite.com and www.walkjogrun.net list a lot of charitable causes across the United States. Other ways I try to incorporate family exercise is to go bicycle riding with my family in the park or on the beach boardwalk and have recently started taking them on hikes. This way you are not only socializing around the table with food and drink but also showing them a healthier life-style that revolves around quality time with the family while getting your heart pumping.

You've heard the saying "Kids do as you do, not as you say?" We are our kids' best role model. If we work out and show our kids how we prioritize it, they will learn to do this too. My mom worked long hours and didn't prioritize working out. When I first started working after college, I too worked long hours, didn't work out and gained 15 pounds my first year on the job. It has taken me many years to figure out that working out is critical to my overall well-being, even if that means I won't be able to spend a lot of time with the kids one night. I try my best to stick to my workout regimen and make sure to let my kids know that exercising is very important and needs to be taken as seriously as other commitments. On those occasions, I usually let my kids go to bed a bit later so that I can squeeze in some extra time with them. My hope is that by seeing this as they grow up, they too will internalize that exercise is a priority that they need to fit into their busy lives, because in reality who really has time to exercise regularly? The key is to make time.

While healthy food and exercise are crucial to our body's well-being, we can't forget our body's need to rest and recharge which we will talk about more extensively in the final body lesson #6.

LESSON #6: INGRAIN IN YOUR KIDS FROM A YOUNG AGE THAT SLEEP IS A GOOD THING.

Just like you need to put the right foods into your body for optimal performance, you also need to give the body the rest it needs in order to recharge. No amount of healthy food is going to compensate for sleep deprivation, yet statistics indicate that our kids are not getting enough sleep these days. First off, sleep has a bad rap and carries a perception of being lazy. When was the last time you just lounged around, rested and did nothing all day? Even if you had the time, it's not very socially acceptable to just lounge around and rest when there is so much to do in so little time. With us putting that pressure on ourselves to be productive, our kids are indirectly learning that as well with all the commitments that we schedule in their lives.

With all these commitments, it is tough for caretakers to get everything done between after school and bed. Eating too close to bedtime hurts sleep patterns as well. Another reason kids are not getting enough sleep is because kids feel like they are missing out when going to sleep. I don't know about you, but I remember feeling that when I was a kid and wanting to stay up as late as possible just for the sake of doing so.

I tend to dangle several "carrots" so to speak as techniques to get my kids to go to sleep at a reasonable hour. They only get extended alone-time with me when I tuck them in if they go to bed on time. When my kids were younger, I'd read them a bedtime story with each one of my kids individually, and they would get to spend 10 exclusive minutes with me before their bedtime. Now that they are a bit older, I still tuck them into bed and have exclusive time with them to meditate, say their positive affirmations (more about both of those items in the Spirit part of this book) and have what we call "pillow talk" (which is when I really hear about what happened during their day). I also dangle the "height carrot." My sons are obsessed with growing tall so I always emphasize how our body repairs itself as we sleep which allows it to grow, and remind them of this when they resist bedtime.

The benefits to sufficient sleep go way beyond not feeling and looking tired. According to health.com, getting the proper amount of sleep improves memory, curbs inflammation, which is linked to conditions like heart disease, stroke, diabetes, etc., and improves athletic and school-grade performance.[35] Well-rested children tend to be more attentive, less hyperactive and impulsive, have better chances of maintaining a healthy weight, and have less stress, less clumsiness, and less depression. That list is enough in itself to get those kids to bed on time.

Sleep deprivation usually equates to weight gain as sleep-deprived people tend to overeat when tired. Lack of sleep affects focus and memory. Also, when you are tired and exhausted you are more prone to bad decision-making.

---

35 Alyssa Sparacino, Alyssa. "11 Surprising Health Benefits of Sleep."Health.com. N.p., n.d. Web. 13 Oct. 2015.
<http://www.health.com/health/gallery/0,,20459221,00.html>.

The number of hours of sleep our kids need, according to The National Sleep Foundation, is listed below:[36] How many hours of sleep per night are your kids getting?

AGE	HOURS OF SLEEP
Newborns	14-17 hours
Infants	12-15 hours
Toddlers	11-14 hours
Preschoolers	10-13 hours
School-Age	9-11 hours
Teenagers	8-10 hours
Young Adults	7-9 hours
Adults	7-9 hours
Older Adults	7-8 hours

---

36 Max Hirshkowitz, PhD, Kaitlyn Whiton, Steven M. Albert, PhD, Cathy Alessi, MD, Oliviero Bruni, MD, Lydia DonCarlos, PhD, Nancy Hazen, PhD, John Herman, PhD, Eliot S. Katz, MD, Leila Kheirandish-Gozal, MD, MSc, David N. Neubauer, MD, Anne E. O'Donnell, MD, Maurice Ohayon, MD, DSc, PhD, John Peever, PhD, Robert Rawding, PhD, Ramesh C. Sachdeva, MD, PhD, JD, Belinda Setters, MD, Michael V. Vitiello, PhD, J. Catesby Ware, PhD, Paula J. Adams Hillard, MD. "National Sleep Foundation's Sleep Time Duration Recommendations: Methodology and Results Summary." Journal of the National Sleep Foundation 1.1 (2015): 40-43. Web. 25 Sept. 2015. <http://www.sleephealthjournal.org/article/S2352-7218 (15)00015-7/abstract>.

There are a few tactics you can use to help kids get the sleep they need. I've incorporated getting to bed on time into the list of chores they need to do in order to get an allowance. Also, when sleep patterns get way off track, for example, in the summer or after a long vacation break, I'll implement a stand-alone reward system for meeting sleep goals for a couple of weeks until they are back on track. I've found that removing my kids' electronic devices from their room at bedtime is crucial to getting a good night's sleep for two reasons. First, this will help avoid the sneaking around to play at night or as kids get older waking up from texts or calls from friends. Second, the bright light from the various screens (iPad, computer, phone, etc.) actually affects melatonin production which can negatively affect our ability to fall asleep.[37]

It is important to keep kids to a consistent waking and sleeping schedule, so while I tend to let kids sleep later and wake up later on weekends, I put a limit on that so that it doesn't interfere too much with their weekly sleep routine. The environment in their rooms can affect sleep as well. I had my kids choose their bedding and pillows to make sure they found it comfortable and excited to get under those blankets at night. I also had night shades installed so that the room stays dark even when the sun rises. The temperature in the house is another factor that can affect sleep, with op-

---

37 Sutherland, Stephani. "Bright Screens Could Delay Bedtime." Scientific American Global RSS. N.p., 19Dec. 2012. Web. 25 Sept. 2015. <http://www.scientificamerican.com/article/bright-screens-could-delay-bedtime/>.

timal temperature being between 68-70 degrees. Finally, eating a large meal right before bed can make it difficult to sleep, so try to avoid that when possible.

This concludes the body section of the book. Having the tools to eat healthy, exercise, and get a good night's sleep. Next, we will be discussing how the mind plays a crucial role in our overall health and well-being.

[3]

Mind

There is a direct correlation between eating a healthy balanced diet, exercising regularly and getting enough sleep, and how it affects our thought patterns, how it makes us feel about ourselves and how we view the world around us. The food we eat doesn't just feed our cells. Food also nourishes our thoughts, which then affect our actions. Now that we know what it takes to get our children's bodies to work better by eating healthier, drinking more water, exercising and sleeping more, we can focus on how to make our children's mindset optimal.

We are all programmed genetically for negative thinking—it's a survival mechanism to make sure we take action in times of need to stay "safe and sound." Did you ever wonder why you never forget any mistake you have made and dwell on them way too long, while you brush off or downplay your accomplishments and successes, attributing them to luck or something that is not a big deal? How we think and our mindset as to how we approach life has a direct correlation with the type of life we are going to have. So it is very important that we retrain our thoughts for success and happiness by focusing on positivity, abundance, giving, gratitude and love.

I still struggle with this, but knowing that everyone goes through it was a huge revelation, an *"aha"* moment for me. Knowing that I'm not alone in these thoughts made me feel less isolated and not as ashamed of them. Like anything in life, awareness is the first step in acknowledging behavior. You cannot alter a behavior without this happening. A big thing I wished I learned growing up is how to approach failure. Please teach your kids how to fail well. If you scour the internet to see what people are writing about when it comes to the word "failure," you'd be pleasantly surprised. The words associated with failure were very positive and even inspiring. Words such as "learning", "great," 'better," "change," "understand," "try", "success", "able", "important" to name a few. To quote my son, Natanel, "A quitter is never a winner."

I grew up thinking that failure was a bad word, and being the cautious person that I am I tried to avoid it at all costs. To me, failure meant I'm not capable, I'm not smart. I'm not worthy. Even if it lead to not trying new things, avoiding some challenges, only taking on what I knew I could succeed in. While that approach pretty much guaranteed I'd succeed in my endeavors, I knew deep down I wasn't pushing myself to my limit and wasn't feeling a lot of passion for what I was doing. I always felt I was fooling everyone into thinking I was smart. I felt like an impostor. I was lucky that in my work environments over the years, my employers saw in me what I didn't always see in myself. Time and time again, I was pushed to take on new challenges beyond my comfort zone and while it petrified me, I knew I had to do it and I pushed forward. After going through a few growing pains, I'd figured out how to get it done and it usually turned out pretty well.

It was through continued exposure to challenges and additional responsibilities that I began to trust and believe in myself more. I started feeling more comfortable when I was faced with new challenges and chartered unknown territory. I learned that when I tried my best no matter what, things will turn out ok. I now know success and failure are one and the same, sharing the same path, not a crossroads like I previously believed. And those that truly failed were the ones who gave up along the way while the successful ones continued forward and persevered despite the obstacles that they faced along the way.

Failure is just life telling you that you are heading in the wrong direction—against your goals. So in reality, failure is just life giving you a nudge to make sure you adjust your course so that you can continue on the right path to achieve your goals. Happiness does not mean you will have no setbacks. It's how you deal with those setbacks and learn from them that cultivate happiness and ultimate success. WE are usually the ones that get in our own way, telling ourselves it's too hard, we are not good enough, we can't do it, etc.

One way to teach kids the lesson about how to view failure and how to overcome fears is through examples of other people's stories. All people that have had success experienced rejection at some point. To drill this home, the kids and I google autobiographies of successful people, especially the ones my kids admire, to show that success came with hard work, failure and continued perseverance. We read these articles to understand what they did to succeed and, as a result, they feel inspired to pursue their own goals.

For example, my younger son is obsessed with soccer. I spent some time googling his favorite players and doing some research on how they got started. For example, one of his favorite soccer players, Lionel Messi, now considered one of the greatest players in our generation, started with very humble beginnings, growing up in a working-class family. Messi was diagnosed with growth hormone deficiency (GHD), a very expensive condition that stunted growth, and put a great financial strain on the family. Reading about how he felt like soccer saved his life and helped him to push through all obstacles to follow his dream, was very inspiring to my son.

Reading inspirational stories with your kids will illustrate how to bounce back from failure, how failure ended up leading to a better outcome and how they can take those same lessons into their own lives. I encourage them to listen to "Ted Talks for Kids." These captivating talks captured on video are meant to be fun and informative while capturing and inspiring young minds. Go to www.ted.com and search for "talks to watch with kids." There you will find a playlist of different videos you can watch with your kids to inspire them. Also, sharing your own stories with your kids on how you dealt with failure in your own life and how you've succeeded can be inspirational to them. It brings you closer since you shared both vulnerable and happy moments with them.

Another life lesson that I wish I learned growing up is that giving to others actually gives you back more than you could imagine. I grew up absorbing the financial stress I felt at home which, as a result, lead me to have a mindset of scarcity, where there isn't enough of anything to go around. Where you need to take what is yours before someone else claims it. Little did I know how much happier I could be if I shifted my mindset from one of scarcity to abundance, and how if you want a certain thing, the best way to get it is to actually give that thing to someone else. For example, I wanted people to donate to a charitable cause I was working on. I was sending all my friends and family notifications about how to donate and I wasn't seeing a lot of donations coming in. When I started feeling a bit discouraged, I received an email about a co-worker friend who wanted to ride his bike across San Francisco to raise money. I donated to his cause the amount that I was asking people to donate to my cause. There is no way to prove whether this worked, but I feel opening that flow of energy is what led to more donations that came in to my cause a few days later.

Giving to others makes you feel good. A great way to get out of the everyday stress and need for perfection is to project energy onto others and enjoy the positive energy

coming to you in return for doing good. Get your kids involved in giving from a young age to ingrain it in their little
bones. Giving a small portion of their allowance to a charity
of their choice is one way to teach this lesson. Doing volun-
teer work can make them feel great and grateful for what
they have. I plan on taking my kids to the soup kitchen to
feed the homeless on Thanksgiving. Getting involved in
community service activities is a great way to teach kids how
to give back to their community. I was just reading about vol-
unteers needed to tag every tree in New York City so that a
tree map of New York City can be created. This would be a
very cool and memorable experience for a family to partake
in.

Teaching empathy is another way to open your children's hearts to giving to others. One way to do this is to try
and consciously be extra nice to people you'd normally ignore or pass by. I was buying water from one of those street
food vendors in New York City and instead of my usual behavior to make a purchase and rush off, I took a few minutes
to ask the cashier how his day was going and to wish him a
successful day. I could see how with everyone rushing about,
he could spend the whole day in contact with other people,
none of whom made any kind of a human connection by asking the simple question "How are you?" Try to put yourself in
someone else's shoes to understand the other side. This is
something where there are many opportunities to teach kids
this lesson. During any conflict they may have with siblings

or friends, I listen intently to what happened from their perspective and then encourage them to think of how the other person would interpret it.

This practice expands their mind beyond the traditional and sometimes trivial way of thinking and has led to a lot more compassion and understanding. Small acts of kindness during the day help your own sense of well-being. Telling a good friend how you appreciate them, asking a friend if they want a piece of your treat, telling someone you like their outfit, are few examples of little things that can go a long way.

Another very important lesson I wished I learned as I was growing up is gratitude and the power it has to really change your mindset and make you happy. Oxford dictionary defines gratitude as "the quality of being thankful; readiness to show appreciation for and to return kindness." [38] In layman's terms, it is to acknowledge the things you are happy for instead of dwelling on the things you don't have. There will always be people who have more, who look better, who are richer, have more friends, have more fun, etc. Don't compare yourself to others. Thinking about how you compare to others will always be a "lose-lose" situation and make you feel unsatisfied when in reality you probably have a pretty good life.

Gratitude is a good way to help curb comparing yourself to others, which will always result in unhappiness

---

38 "Gratitude." Gratitude: Definition of Gratitude in Oxford Dictionary (American English) (US). Oxford, n.d. Web. 01 Nov. 2015. <http://www.oxforddictionaries.com/us/definition/american_english/gratitude>.

and dissatisfaction. When you catch yourself doing that, try to actively change your perspective from what you don't have to what you do have. Let me tell you a story about how I worked with my older son to alter his mindset before going to camp. We found out a few days before camp that two out of the four kids who weren't nice to him last summer were going to be in his group again. He started telling me the story, upset that he will need to deal with these two kids again. In our conversation, I said, "It sounds like good news over last year that two of the kids that weren't nice to you are not in your group this year. And the other two that are, you can treat this summer as a new beginning and try to be nice to everybody. And if they aren't nice again, try to ignore them."

Turns out one of those kids he is now friends with and the other kid, while still not great, doesn't pick on him anymore. I was happy to hear that and told him that I really think by retraining his mindset with gratitude, he projected the positive energy required to have a happy experience at camp.

On a weekly basis, I make a list with the kids of things we are grateful for to start out the week. I usually start the conversation by asking them if they feel like they are lucky and ask them to list what they are happy and grateful for. I then talk to them about their list when I put them to bed every night, and ask them if there are any new things to add to the list. This way they go to bed on a positive note which I feel probably makes them sleep better through the night. I recently started a happiness journal with the kids. I did this by taking my kids to buy a blank journal so that they'd have ownership in choosing one with a cover they liked.

I then went on to one of my favorite inspirational sites, Marc & Angel Hack Life (www.marcandangel.com) and printed their article called "50 Happiness Quotes to Change the Way You Think" and cut out each quote and taped one quote per page. Then on a regular basis (I try daily but we miss days here and there when things get busy), we read one of the quotes and then I ask each of my boys to write anything that comes to mind after reading it. For example, the first quote listed is "It only takes one person to make you happy and change your life: *you.*" I first read the quote without saying *"you"* and asked them to fill in the blank and why. You don't have to use these quotes but can pull anything that will inspire you and your children to have impactful conversations about happiness.

Now let's talk about how teaching accountability, positivity, and abundance can be a great boost to the inner workings of the mind. Starting with accountability, whether or not an outcome is positive or negative, I encourage my children to take ownership and accountability for their behavior and actions. I'm trying to make sure they avoid being prone to have "victim" behavior, where nothing is their fault and anything bad is caused by external circumstances. Victim behavior keeps your mind trapped in that negativity since you feel you can't change or control something that was done to you. I want my kids to grow up knowing that they are the master of their own destiny. Our thoughts create actions, which create our future.

Trying to be positive even when times are tough, and trying to learn the lessons for growth when things don't go as planned can make kids more resilient to the bad times in life. If I see that my child is not looking at something in a positive way, I ask him to take a pause and think about if they are looking at a particular situation with the glass "half full or half empty." I try to show them how they can look at the same situation with a half full perspective. I encourage them to try and see what lessons they can take to help them learn and apply to this and future situations. Even if they don't change their mindset, seeing alternate ways of looking at the same scenario can help train their mind long-term to be able to do this same exercise on their own as they grow up.

As I stated earlier in this book, when I was young, I was taught to have a "scarcity" mindset since I grew up feeling the financial stress at home. I still struggle with this since things learned early in life are so ingrained in our mind and it's tough to retrain our thinking. I've been working hard on changing my perspective from scarcity to abundance and trying to teach my kids this at an early age so that I don't project my childhood mentality onto them and they don't struggle with it like I did. Abundance is defined as an overflowing amount, a feeling that you have more than enough for yourself and others. To achieve this, you first need to take care of yourself—mind, body and soul, the basic tenants of this book. You also have to teach your children to have faith and trust that things happen when they are intended to happen, sometimes for reasons we cannot begin to comprehend. I really believe that everything happens for a reason, even when it doesn't seem like it at the time. And then, as the expression goes, you need to "fake it until you make it." So acting as if you already have abundance will bring that flow into your life. This can even take shape in the words we use both out loud and in our thoughts. Thanking the universe for your success even before it happens will put the energy out into the universe to make it happen. As I was writing this book, I thanked the universe for writing a book that is changing people's lives even before anyone bought the book.

I was contemplating making a big purchase that I could afford but was very hesitant to spend the money because of my scarcity prone mindset: If I spend that amount of money it would be gone forever. When I became aware of these thoughts, I asked myself, if I already felt abundant would I hesitate to buy this item that I knew would bring my family and me a lot of joy? Since the answer was no, I moved forward to buy it and I am so happy that I did. If you want something but have no idea how to get it, teach your kids to give what they desire and the universe will repay them in multiples.

An example of how I worked through this abundant change of mindset was with my older son as he was entering the new school year. He found out that none of his good friends were going to be in his new class. He would only have one acquaintance and a kid who picked on him a couple years back. He was not looking forward to school and asked me if I could get his class changed. I spoke to him about how to look at his situation with a different, more positive per-spective. I assured him that his good friends in the other class will always be his friends, and asked him to try and re-alize that now he has an opportunity to meet a whole new set of friends in his new class. We then discussed how this kid who picked on him two years ago may have been going through a hard time back then (his parents were going through a divorce) and not to assume he will be like that again. I asked him to have a positive, open mindset going into class. I reassured him that everyone confronted with this situation would feel the same way he does. I advised him to "kill him with kindness." And if he wasn't jiving well with this kid, to ignore him and act happy no matter what. After a tough couple of weeks getting adjusted to the new class, teacher and course work, he began to make new friends and in no time he had a new group of friends, including the kid that picked on him in the past.

Happiness can only be achieved in the present mo-ment. Too many of us think that once we reach this or that goal, then we will be happy. One that I used to always tell my-self is that if I won the lotto, then I'd be eternally happy. Re-alizing the chances of that are slimmer than being hit by lightning, I made a conscious decision not to wait for that or what it really meant, reaching that financial freedom I so yearned for from childhood. And be happy--not yesterday, not tomorrow, but today! That is why regardless of the end-goal, I try to focus on the process with my kids. People usu-ally only see and focus on the end-result and wait for that to bring happiness. The processes you go through and sacrifices you make to achieve the end result, must also fulfill you.

My older son is on the swim team. This past year he had a goal to break one of the records for either of the two strokes he excelled in: butterfly or freestyle. He used to come home from practice miserable and upset each time he didn't get closer to breaking the record, wanting it so badly and feeling that once he achieved this he would be so happy and accomplished. I spoke to him and told him that it would feel great if and when he break a record, but he can't approach each practice and swim meet with that pressure. He had to relax, remember why he loved swimming in the first place and try, just try his best. Things would take care of themselves in due time. Happiness can be achieved from a simple change of perception. He still hasn't broken any records but is enjoying his swim practices more. Gratitude can almost magically make you feel happier. The sheer act of feeling grateful for what you have, no matter how bad things get, is always the way to go.

The most impactful lesson about a healthy mindset is one I owe to my amazing sister, Natalie, who taught me:

"FEAR IS NOT REAL. It is simply your perspective based on the story you created in your mind."

FEAR is an acronym in the English language for "False Evidence Appearing Real." We all create our own stories based on our life experiences, both positive and negative. Since we each have our own unique life experience, our stories are also unique to us. You can be having a conversation with someone and both of you can leave that conversation with a different impression, a different story. A lot of arguments stem from each person putting their own perspective and weight/value to the words they hear and reacting accordingly. Since most of this occurs at a subconscious level, it is key is to be aware of it to begin to understand what is going on and start to isolate the stories you are bringing into your fears and disagreements. Once you isolate it, you see that those stories which may have served a purpose in the past, are no longer valid and are now holding you back.

An example of this is my husband's "story" he created about his aptitude for math. When he was in 5th grade, he got pneumonia and was out of school for three weeks. His class started learning how to multiply and divide decimals, and by the time he got back to class he was very much behind. Neither his teacher nor his school made it a priority to get him caught up. His parents, who were immigrants to the country, were at work all the time and didn't make sure their son was making up all missed work. As a result, he got further and further behind to the point where he was no longer able to catch up. From that year forward his "story" in his head was that he was bad in math and stopped trying. Years later he found himself in the real estate industry needing to quickly assess whether a property was worth buying and then selling. He was very quick to figure out all the numbers and was pretty close to budget on most of his deals. Not letting his childhood "story" hold him back was instrumental to his success in this industry.

If you have fear in your mind as you try to make a decision, you will never choose what is ultimately best for you. Using the tenet that fear is not real, we begin to understand that if you change your thoughts, you change your reality. Change the story in your head and you will change your perception. This theory has helped me improve my decision-making mindset and now I'm starting to teach my kids. Relinquish control and defer to the universe to help you make decisions, having faith that all is good with the universe, ask the universe to guide you. If my kids have a big decision to make and are unsure of what to do, before bed I ask them to close their eyes, say the two options they are weighing and then just relax their mind asking the universe to help them make a decision. In the following days, the calmness of releasing that power to the universe enabled them to think more clearly about what the options were and which of those was the best option for them.

As the life coach, thought leader and author Marie Forleo says, "Everything that is figureoutable makes you unstoppable."[39]

Knowing that you have what you need within you to figure anything out should give you peace of mind. In general, if you have doubts about something and need to make a decision, I recommend a simple meditation on the issue at hand with your breathing relaxed and your mind clear. I will delve more into meditation in the next section of the book—Spirit. The answer might be closer than you think. When a

---

39 Forleo, Maria. "All About the inside Scoop." RSS. Maria Forleo, 2015. Web. 13 Oct. 2015. <http://www.marieforleo.com/about/the-company/>.

decision is made from a calm and rationale place, it will be made based on clarity, not fear. I like to tell my kids that we are all buckets of energy. Do you fill that bucket with positive or negative energy? What is the story we are telling ourselves and do we want to change our story? The answer to these questions can change the course of your life and happiness.

Let's now shift our discussion to more of the practical lessons I learned that can help with our mind and harnessing the power to get things done. A great set of skills to teach your children are project management skills. According to the Project Management Institute, "Project management, is the application of knowledge, skills, tools, and techniques to project activities to meet the project requirements." In layman's terms this means how to get things done when you need it done by, and within budget. Anything in a kid's life or school can be called a project. A project might be as simple as creating a lemonade stand in the summer, doing a school science project, to more advanced projects like tackling the college application process.

I've been a project manager for over 10 years and it is those skills that enabled me to manage a $20 million dollar project portfolio for my company's largest Fortune 100 account. These skills are what propelled me to finish this book while working full-time and raising two kids.

Time management skills are key to getting anything done. Any project can seem daunting and overwhelming in the beginning. This usually leads to procrastination or not doing the project at all. Procrastination often stems from fear of failure. The key to approaching anything, whether it's big or small, is to chunk it into small, actionable steps. This way you only need to focus on one step at a time. Even if you don't know all the steps, it's okay. As long as you list in written form as many steps and activities as you know, this can help you plan into the future. As you start completing steps in the project, you will have more knowledge and be able to fill in those gaps organically. It's kind of funny and almost embarrassing to share, but this chunking skill came to be very natural from a very young age. When I would get my course syllabus, I would look at everything that had to be done in the semester and "chunk out" what I had to do and by when so that I was able to get things done without stressing out about it. This tactic enabled me to never need to pull an all-nighter in college, and allowed me to graduate with honors from a top 10 university. A way to put this into practice in your homes is to look at your children's agenda/syllabus for the semester and guide them through this thinking, working backwards from test dates, so that they can start training their mind to think in an organized chunking fashion.

A big part of project management is staying within budget. Teaching kids about budgeting from an early age can drastically affect how they are with money in adulthood. Due to financial hardships I experienced in my childhood, I learned the hard way the stress that can be caused by a lack of money. I vowed to live differently, even if it meant living simply as long as it was within my means so that I could have peace of mind and enjoy life. Since my children are fortunate enough not to live in that same stressful environment, I have to artificially create an environment for them to learn about and respect the value of money, and teach them the balance on how to save it, spend it and donate it. I start off by giving my kids a weekly allowance that is tied to a chores chart. Chores range from easy to difficult and I even give them a few bonus options to make some extra dough. I opened a bank savings account under their name where I had them deposit a portion of the money. Since I don't want to raise a bunch of Mr. Crabs (SpongeBob anyone?), I also encourage them to spend a portion of their money and to donate some, as well.

I recommend that they save 40% of their money, donate 10% and spend the remaining 50% on things that bring them joy, fun and great life experiences. For example, I put both my kids in day camp this summer. I don't know how camps are in your neck of the woods, but when I came to know how much day camps cost, I was shocked. Being that both my husband and I work full-time and all of their friends are in camp, we made the necessary sacrifices throughout the year and signed them up. We then found out that they have an optional overnight special trip (3 days/two nights) within camp for an additional $500. I told my kids I wasn't going to sign them up, explaining how we spent enough for camp, etc. My kids understood and were grateful for being able to go to this camp. Then, two days before the overnight, my older son had a playdate with one of his friends who told him that it's not too late to sign up and that all his friends were going and begged him to go. My son understood that if he wanted to go he would have to make a significant contribution to it (on principle). Once I got him to be ok paying for it all, I surprised him by saying we'd split it with him. He was beyond ecstatic that he didn't have to use all his money to go and at the same time he was very appreciative and understood the value of the trip—having used a good chunk of his own money.

How do you know what a worthy project or endeavor is to put your time, energy and resources into? It should align with the end-goals you or your child ultimately want to achieve. Whether that is scoring a goal in next week's soccer match, saving up money to buy a video game or getting a good grade in this year's science project. It's important to have goals and to state them out loud and on paper so that the energy is put out there in the universe to help achieve them. When helping my kids figure out their goals, I use what I learned in the corporate world. First step is to define SMART goals. A **"SMART"** goal is defined as a goal that is **S**pecific, **M**easurable, **A**chievable, **R**esults-focused, and **T**ime-bound."

S - It should be clearly written and defined so you know exactly what you want to do.

M - It should be measurable so you know when you have achieved the goal.

A - It should be achievable and challenge you slightly, but never be out of reach.

R - It should measure results and outcomes, not activities.

T - It should have a clear timeframe for achieving the desired goal.

It's not realistic in our very busy hectic lives to do this very often. To take again from the corporate world, I try to do this once a year, usually at the beginning of the school year when the kids are all jazzed up to start anew. I then try to look at those goals again with them mid-point into the semester, to see how they are tracking and then follow the process again for the second semester.

Now that we've covered both the ideological and practical areas of helping our children have an optimal mindset for success, let's talk about spirituality.

[4]

Spirit

I believe spirituality is focusing outward, knowing something greater than yourself is out there—something that maybe even created you and sustains you. Spirituality is a posture of gratitude and awareness. To focus less on the self, the ego, and more on "What is my purpose? What am I here for? Who am I?" If you scour the Internet, you will notice that there is no single agreed-upon definition of spirituality. Anything that can be viewed as meaningful can be classified as spiritual. For some it's religion, for others yoga, for even others spirituality is simply living life being true to oneself.

In order to be open to what comes with spirituality, you need to be able to calm your mind and be receptive to what comes through. I believe that there is a higher power (or energy) helping to guide us on this earth and we have to be in tune with it for it to happen.

Meditation is a very effective way to calm the mind; it is common for our mind to doubt itself. Meditation trains the mind to be available to anything that arises. It is a wonderful tool used to seek enlightenment and guide you to find inner peace. Meditation can be hard and frustrating in the beginning, since it can be very hard to quiet your mind, especially when you are so used to being productive. We live in a world of multi-tasking; we are overstimulated by social media and even find it hard to disconnect from work when we go on vacation. It can almost feel tortuous to force yourself to be still and try to remove all your everyday thoughts that naturally enter your mind at a rate of a mile a minute. You may feel like you are wasting your time when you try to stop and meditate.

Why go through this initial frustration most of us experience when we first start meditating? Well, because of all the amazing benefits, of course! Regular meditation practice reduces stress and aging. It increases attention span and immune system. It improves sleep, brain function and makes you feel happier and more connected to those around you. Meditation leads to having a more open mind that is more prone to being able to come up with creative solutions. It increases your energy, improves your metabolism and helps in weight loss. Do you need to hear any more?

It's ideal to meditate 20 minutes a day and you usually see the results after 8 weeks of regular meditation practice. Now, I know how hard it is to find the time every day. Most of the time life gets in the way and you just can't find those 20 free minutes. Do not fret. Even if you don't have time to meditate 20 minutes every day, try to find even a couple of minutes a day to still your mind and to connect with your inner self. The key here is to make this into a daily habit regardless of how many minutes you have and eventually it will become a part of your daily routine. Once it becomes a habitual part of your day, you will actually look forward to doing it longer.

Everyone can learn how to meditate. You can choose to go to school to learn how to meditate. You can take a course online, read books, etc. There are many different schools on different techniques of how to meditate and I listed a few resources for you below. The bottom line is that meditation is the practice of quieting the mind and gaining self-awareness through focusing on one's breathing.

To make sure you are getting the most out of meditating, while laying the foundation to make it a habit, pick a time of day that works and try to keep it to that timeframe as much as possible. For me, the best time to do this with my kids is right before bedtime. That way, there is nothing else I need to get done with them afterward and it puts them in a relaxed state right before going to sleep. Also, consider the environment, making it as relaxing as possible so that it's easier to focus and not be distracted by outside stimulus.

Here is one technique I teach my kids when it comes to meditating. This technique is used by Japanese Buddhist monks:

- Starting with a few deep breaths prior to meditation also helps you relax and prepare to get into a deeper meditative state.

- Start by either lying down or sitting down comfortably. Once you have found your position, try NOT to move until meditation practice is over.
- Focus your breath inward and relax your body.
- Inhale slowly a long and full breath first, filling your abdomen and allowing your diaphragm to expand, followed by your lungs, to the point where there is no more room to breathe further.
- Hold your breath for a count of 4 seconds.
- Slowly release your breath by exhaling first from your lungs then through your abdomen until there is no more air left in you.
- Repeat this series for the duration of your meditation practice.

Your mind is like a restless child and you may find that it wanders off. Every time that happens, acknowledge the thought and direct your mind back to focusing on your breathing. When you finish meditation, open your eyes gently and slowly so that you can peacefully become aware of yourself and your surroundings.

I introduced meditation to my kids by doing it with them before I put them to bed. I had us all lay down in bed, softly closing our eyes and started focusing on our breathing. Expanding your diaphragm (sticking your stomach out) on the inhale, and contracting your diaphragm on the exhale. I put on one of Oprah and Deepak's meditation audio recordings. Before I pressed play, I let them know that they should just listen to what they will be hearing, and try to focus on repeating the mantra, clearing all other thoughts from their minds. My younger son, who is only eight years old, wanted me to stop the recording and start it over again four times because he had so much trouble clearing his mind. He was surprised at the number of unrelated thoughts that were entering his mind. I reassured him that this is normal and that it will take a while to achieve this state and to just go through meditation practice from start to finish, doing the best that he could. Afterward, I noticed he fell asleep a lot quicker than he usually did. I was happy that even though he was a bit frustrated that he couldn't master meditation on his first go that he wanted to do it again.

There are many meditation resources out there for you to explore. The Meditation Society offers 108 meditations on their website http://meditationsociety.com/108meds.html.

Oprah and Deepak offer free meditations online centered on manifesting different things over a 21-day period, the time it takes to acquire a habit. The recent one I participated in and really enjoyed with the kids was called the "21-day manifesting grace through gratitude". There are also many free and paid apps you can download on your smartphone.

List of general mediation apps:

- Headspace - free (iOS, android, amazon)
- Insight timer - free (iOS, android)
- Stop, breathe & think - free (iOS, android)
- Breathe2Relax - free (iOS, android)
- Mindfulness meditation - free (android), $1.99 (iOS)
- Simply being - $1.99 cents (iOS, android)
- The mindfulness app $2.99 (iOS, android)
- Buddhify - $4.99 (iOS, android)

Specific to kids, but for adults too

- Smiling mind - free (iPad, iPhone)
- Sleep Meditations for Kids, by Christiane Kerr: Calming Bedtime Relaxation Stories- free (iOS)
- Relax Melodies - Sleep zen sounds & white noise for meditation, yoga and baby relaxation- free (iOS)
- Take a Chill - Stressed Teens ($1.99, iOS)
- The mindfulness app - $2.99 (iOS, Android)

Another positive activity that can be incorporated while meditating or on its own is affirmations. Affirmations are positive statements about who we are, and what we can become and experience. Positive self-talk or affirmations are used to help you feel better, create positive attitudes and achieve desired goals. The underlying premise here is we are what we think, and what we think we end up creating, whether we know it or not. Since our minds are prone to negative thinking and self-doubt, this can translate to non-optimal outcomes that then feed into this vicious cycle of negative thinking and actions. Since kids from a young age are so impressionable and are a sponge to anything you teach them, it is ideal to introduce affirmations into daily life early on.

I strive to make daily affirmations a habit in my family. Repeating positive affirmations with your kids first thing in the morning can start their day off on the right foot. Before bed can also help ensure they have sweet dreams and wake up happy and refreshed. Also, repeating it throughout the day when you need that extra boost can further reinforce its effects. The key is repetition, since it is through the power of repetition that you will start to rewire your brain, changing the way you think and consequently the way you behave. Even if you don't believe the affirmation when you say it, don't fret. After ongoing repetition over time, you actually will start to believe it and these affirmations will eventually come true.

To introduce the idea of affirmations, I helped my kids create an affirmations vision board. I first printed out a long list of affirmations (see the next page for a sample of them) and cut out each one. I then took my kids to a craft store to buy poster board, markers, paint and other decorations. I spread out the list of cut-out affirmations on the table and asked my kids to pick the ones that they instinctively felt the need to pick up and could relate to wanting more in their life. Then based on the affirmations they pulled, I asked them what visual image they associated with them. Once they had the list of images to associate with selected affirmations, they googled images of those visualizations and printed them. Alternately, they could draw or paint the visual as well. They pasted the affirmations and images on the poster board and then added any other decorations to it to further personalize it. We hung their boards in the room where they could look at them every day.

Another way to incorporate affirmations in a creative way is through the use of affirmation flash cards. I start the same way I did with vision boards by printing a list of curated affirmations and cutting each one out separately. I then worked with the kids to glue one positive affirmation statement onto one flashcard and decorate the card with visualization they associate with it, whether that be an image we found online or a hand-drawn image. Since the kids had a big hand in created these flashcards, they took more ownership and were more willing and excited to pick a card as a daily ritual and read it. They are actually curious to see which card they will get and usually pick a few before putting the deck away.

Below is a list of affirmations I do with kids. While this is just a sampling of ones that I curated and that work well in my household. You can find one of the largest collections of positive affirmations at www.freeaffirmations.org.

- I approve of myself.
- I love myself unconditionally.

- I accept what is, I let go of what was and I have faith in what will be.
- I accept myself even though I sometimes make mistakes.
- I absorb knowledge like a sponge and am able to apply what I have learned.
- I believe I can be whatever I want to be.
- I am proud of myself for even daring to try; most people don't even do that.
- I am a good kid.
- I believe in myself and my abilities.
- I enjoy being, feeling and thinking positive.
- I am willing to learn something new every day.
- I believe in me.
- Today will be an awesome day.
- I am stronger than any excuse.
- Ideas for problem-solving come easily and quickly to me.
- I have unlimited potential.
- I am loved.
- I am capable.
- I accept and approve of myself exactly how I am.
- Today and every day I am so thankful.
- I am awesome.
- Don't let anyone change who you are.
- I am a good reader.
- I am a fast learner.

- I am smart.
- I am full of good ideas.
- I am perfect just the way I am.
- I am safe.
- Every problem has an answer.
- I am kind to others and they are kind to me.
- I express myself clearly.
- I make friends easily.
- I am a good listener.
- I am healthy.
- I am strong.
- I love my body.

Another vessel into spirituality is through proper breathing. Most people go about their day not really breathing as nature intended. We apparently breathe an average of 20,000 times a day without giving it a second thought, but that doesn't mean we are doing it correctly.

What does breathing the right way even mean and why does it matter? Breathing correctly means that our bodies are receiving enough oxygen, which in turn ensures that our brain and other vital organs are getting essential nutrients. When we don't breathe correctly, it can affect us both physically and emotionally. We can feel tired, lethargic, and have issues with our skin and muscles. On an emotional level, it can cause insomnia, panic attacks, anxiety, sadness, and depression.

As babies, we were all born knowing the correct way to breathe, so it's in all of us. If you watch a baby while they sleep, you will notice they take slow and relaxing breaths from their abdomen, not from their chest. This is called belly breathing. Belly breathing increases lung capacity. All the demands and stress of everyday life has put us into more of a fight or flight mode way of breathing, where breathing is shallow and short, emanating from the chest instead of the abdomen. The way you belly-breathe is to inhale air into your belly slowly but steadily as if you are filling up a balloon. Then hold your breath for about three seconds to give your lung time to absorb the fresh air within and then exhale slowly. It is recommended that you practice belly breathing with your children as often as possible so that it can become second nature to them. It is ideal to practice belly-breathing seated on the floor in a cross-legged position since that will also open up your hips, build core strength, etc. If this position is too uncomfortable try sitting in a chair or even lying down. Signing your kids up for kids' yoga classes can help both with practicing belly-breathing as well as improve flexibility through the yoga poses.

A very powerful breathing technique I learned from Andrew Weil, who is a doctor, teacher, and bestselling author on holistic health, is called the 4-7-8 technique.[40] It is a powerful anti-anxiety measure and can even help deal with unwanted cravings. I've taught this technique to my kids and encouraged them to use it when they feel stressed out or anxious. My son usually gets very anxious before taking a test.

---

40 Weil M.D., Andrew. "Videos." Dr. Weil's Breathing Exercises: 4-7-8 Breath. Weil Lifestyle, 2015. Web. 13 Oct. 2015.
<http://www.drweil.com/drw/u/VDR00160/Dr-Weils-Breathing-Exercises-4-7-8-Breath.html>.

This led him to take the test very slowly and triple check his answers, but then he could not get through the entire exam in the allotted time. Performing the 4-7-8 breathing technique before his exam has made him more relaxed and able to take exams in a calmer fashion, which has led to better test scores.

So how do you do the 4-7-8 technique? To prep for it, get in a comfortable position and have your tongue touch the roof of your mouth. Breathe in through your nose quietly. Then blow out through your mouth forcefully, letting all the air out. Breathe in through your nose slowly for 4 seconds. Then hold your breath in for 7 seconds. Finally, release your breath out for 8 seconds forcefully. Repeat this for 4 cycles twice a day, morning and night for a total of 8 cycles per day at most. Doing it more than 8 cycles may cause dizziness. If you do this for 6-8 weeks, you will witness remarkable changes as this breathing technique has the power to change the tone of the nervous system.

I went to the beach with some friends recently and my friend's seven-year-old daughter told her mom that she has a tummy ache from being worried. Her mom asked her what she was worried about and she replied that she worries about a lot about different things. I then chimed in asking my son if he can teach her the 4-7-8 breathing technique. I figured if it was a kid teaching a kid, she would be more receptive. Not only did she do it but she loved it, giggling along the way. The other kids we came with caught wind of what they were doing and tried it as well. The moms were happy to learn this tip and were excited to try this to see how it worked.

[5]

Conclusion

After sharing all the things I learned as it relates to mind, body and spirit, my hope is that you feel like you have the tools and resources to start incorporating the things you have learned into your and your family's lives. If you are feeling like this might seem like a lot to take on, I encourage you to find a few things or even just one thing to start with and then move in baby steps. If change is too drastic, it can get overwhelming and hard to make into a daily part of your life. So reflect about which lessons made the most impact on you and try to take something small to incorporate into your family's routine. And then once that becomes a habit, pick something else and so on, and so forth. For example, for my older son, I started by first teaching him about portion control while incorporating more veggies into his diet to offset the smaller portion of other food types. For my younger son, I started by teaching him about sugar and worked with him on ways to cut that down one step at a time, while sneaking in veggies any way I could so that he could start acquiring a taste for them. And for me, I learned how to meditate and I am trying to make that into a daily habit since I definitely feel a difference on the days that I meditate.

We all need balance and harmony in life to be our happiest. I truly believe that balance is found through moderation while enjoying the most life has to offer. When our body is in balance it can best heal itself, when our mind is in balance it can think most clearly and make good decisions, when our spirit is in balance it can best guide us to achieve our life's purpose.

Balance and harmony with your body means a whole host of things. When it comes to balance in food like I've said before, I follow the 80/20 rule. The 80% comes with things I can more easily control. This applies to most of the groceries I buy. I also try to provide my kids with home-cooked meals during the school/work week. This then allows me more freedom to splurge a bit more on weekends when we eat out (at least a couple of times). Even when we go out some of the time, I try to stay within these guidelines—for example, staying away from meat or poultry that might not be of the highest quality. And other times, I just go all out, knowing it's so seldom, and for me that is okay. This is my balance, but it's up to you to find your own balance. Maybe it's tough to do all home-cooked meals during the week, so you splurge on some of those days when you have back-to-back extracurricular activities with the kids, and cook more when you have time on weekends.

Balance in exercise for my family comes with exercising at a level we can maintain on a pretty consistent basis. For me, that is 2-4 times a week incorporating both high-intensity workouts, like spin and kickboxing, with lower-impact core strengthening and flexibility workouts, like yoga or Pilates. For my kids, we follow the same frequency of 2-4 times per week doing sports they enjoy—swimming and tennis for my older son and soccer and basketball for my younger son. When you exercise too much, it can lead to injuries and wear and tear on the body that over time can cause irreparable damage.

Balance in sleep is very important as well. We want to have enough energy to tackle the day ahead. At the same time, we don't want to miss out on an occasional night out because we need a certain amount of hours of sleep per night. So I follow the 80/20 rule there as well, trying to get my kids to bed on time most nights and allow them to stay up later when we have special occasions that I want them to enjoy.

Balance and harmony in mind to me means following the lessons of positivity while maintaining a sense of realism. To incorporate the theory of abundance without being excessive or wasteful. To be giving while making sure to still take care of myself. To be grateful for everything I have while striving for more. To feel the fear and do it anyway, but not if what is being asked is to metaphorically "jump off a cliff without a parachute." To learn project management skills to help get things done, while allowing for spontaneity and some down time. Learning to live more in the moment, but not at the expense of failing to plan ahead or foregoing lessons learned in the past.

Balance in spirituality means finding meaning in your life without being a fanatic or possessed by it. It is incorporating this happy bliss into your life in a way that feels healthy and freeing versus limiting and all-consuming. I follow the 80/20 rule here as well. As much as I'd love to meditate every day and say all my positive affirmations every day, breathe using my belly every day, pray every day and feel my purpose every day, that's not real life. And I don't want to beat myself about it when everyday life gets in the way. So I strive to do as much as I can and am grateful and thankful for everything I can do, since every little bit counts and adds up to a bigger whole over time.

My wish for you is that after reading this book, you have the body, mind and spirit tools to find your own balance. And that you feel inspired and confident to teach your children the tools to find their balance, harmony and happiness as they continue on this lovely journey called life.

Special Note to My Reader:

Thank you for taking the time to read my book. If it was beneficial and had a positive impact on you, please share it with another Busy Mom.

For more helpful tips on how to improve the lives of your kids, please visit me at BusyMomsCheatSheet.com and follow Busy Mom's Cheat Sheet on Facebook and Instagram.

I would be very grateful for a review on Amazon and look forward to your feedback. Let's all learn and grow together.

XO, Lilly

#LillyCadoch #BusyMomsCheatSheet

[6]

Appendix: 45 Recipes

These recipes in the pages below are tried and true winners in my household. They are geared to getting your kids to eat healthy in a gradual way by slowly phasing out bad foods and replacing them with better foods.

BREAKFAST

BERRY DELICIOUS SMOOTHIE

This berry delicious smoothie is a hit with both of my picky eaters at home. Protein powder makes it extra filling and nutritious.

Yield: Serves 2

Ingredients
- ½ cup yogurt (organic vanilla preferable)
- 1 cup milk (organic, whole grass-fed preferable)
- ½ cup berries (any type, prefer strawberry) frozen or fresh
- 1 tbsp. honey
- 1 fig (frozen) or date
- 1 tbsp. peanut powder (or 2 tbsp. almond butter)
- 1 tbsp. hemp protein powder

Directions:
Add all ingredients to a blender and blend until smooth.

COCONUT BERRY SMOOTHIE

This smoothie is dairy free, a good source of omega 3s, tropical and makes me feel like I'm on vacation.

Yield: Serves 2

Ingredients
- ½ cup coconut milk
- ½ cup almond milk
- ½ cup berries (any type, prefer strawberry) frozen or fresh
- Handful of spinach leaves
- 1 tbsp. honey
- 1 tbsp. flaxseed
- 1 tbsp. hemp protein powder or hemp seed

Directions:
Add all ingredients to a blender and blend until smooth.

BERRY NUTTY SMOOTHIE

The cashews in this smoothie recipe make it super creamy and filling.

Yield: Serves 2

Ingredients
- 1 cup milk (organic, whole grass-fed preferable) or non-dairy milk of your choice
- 1 banana
- 1 cup mixed berries frozen or fresh (preferably organic, dirty dozen fruit)
- 1 cup yogurt (organic vanilla preferable)
- 1 tbsp. honey and/or 1 date to sweeten
- 1 tbsp. flaxseed
- 1 tbsp. hemp protein powder or hemp seed
- ¼ cup cashew nuts

Directions:
Add all ingredients to a blender and blend until smooth.

CHOCOLATE BANANA SMOOTHIE

This smoothie tastes too good to be healthy.

Yield: Serves 2

Ingredients
- 1 cup milk (organic, whole grass-fed preferable) or non-dairy milk of your choice
- 1 banana
- 1 tbsp. peanut powder or almond butter
- 1 cup yogurt (organic vanilla preferable)
- 1 tbsp. honey and/or 1 date to sweeten
- 1 tbsp. coconut oil
- 1 tbsp. oatmeal
- 1 tbsp. chocolate chips
- 1 tbsp. flaxseed

Directions:
Add all ingredients to a blender and blend until smooth.

CHEESY VEGGIE OMELET

This protein vegetable-rich breakfast fuels your kids with the energy they need to start their morning on the right foot.

Yield: Serves 3-4

Ingredients
- 6 eggs, scrambled in bowl
- 1 tbsp. organic whole milk
- ¼ cup tomatoes, diced
- ¼ cup mushrooms, diced
- ¼ cup spinach, chopped
- ¼ cup bell pepper, diced
- ¼ cup onion, diced (optional)
- 2 tbsp. olive oil
- 2 tbsp. cheese (feta, mozzarella or cheddar)
- Salt to taste

Directions:
Add oil to skillet on medium heat and sauté vegetables, starting with onion, then every minute add another vegetable. After onions are translucent, add pepper, then tomatoes, mushrooms and finally spinach. Scramble eggs in a bowl with the milk and season with a sprinkle of salt. Add the eggs to the skillet with sautéed vegetables. When the eggs have set on the bottom, lift the edges and tilt the pan to allow the uncooked egg to flow under to cook. When eggs are set sprinkle

with cheese and then fold omelet in half. Once cheese melts, slide onto a plate and serve.

WHOLESOME HEARTWARMING OATMEAL

This recipe is super quick to prep the night before, leaving you with a balanced breakfast in the morning in minutes.

Yield: Serves 3-4

Ingredients
- 1 cup old-fashioned oats
- 2 cups almond milk
- ½ shredded apple (preferably organic)
- 2 tbsp. slivered almonds
- 2 tbsp. golden raisins or cranberries
- 1 tbsp. honey or maple syrup
- 1 tsp vanilla extract
- 1 tsp cinnamon
- ¼ cup sliced strawberries (optional)

Directions:
Mix all ingredients together. Let soak overnight. Heat on medium and cook 10 minutes, stirring frequently. Garnish with fresh strawberries and serve.

LUNCH

1. Dinner leftovers - I try to make an extra portion of dinner so that I can pack the kids leftovers for lunch the next day in a thermos.

2. The combination of a couple of snacks listed on the snack recipe ideas on pages 134-135. For example, hummus and pita chips with a smoothie.

3. Quesadilla - There are so many varieties you can make here. Some of my kids' favorites are cheese, black bean and cheese, chicken and cheese, and cheese and guacamole.

4. Egg salad with lettuce, tomato on whole-wheat bread, pita or wrap.

5. Tuna salad with lettuce, tomato on whole-wheat bread, pita or wrap

6. Sliced chicken or turkey breast with lettuce, tomato on whole-wheat bread, pita or wrap.

7. PB&H wrap - Assemble peanut or other nut butter, sliced banana and a drizzle of honey on a wrap.

8. Meatball sandwich using leftovers from sweet & sour meatball recipe.

DINNER

Preparing a healthy dinner for your family can be stressful, but it doesn't have to be. The recipes in this section are fast, easy and please even the pickiest bellies in my house.

ZUCCHINI SPAGHETTI PASTA

I started gardening this summer and, fortunately, have had an abundance of zucchini. My kids are pasta-lovers, so instead of making the traditional spaghetti dish, I was able to cut out ½ of the carbs in this dish by spiralizing zucchini with the pasta.

Yield: 1-2 servings
Ingredients
- Spaghetti, enough strands to be the size of a quarter
- 1 Zucchini, spiralized into spaghetti-like strands
- Dash of garlic powder
- Dash of salt
- 1 tbsp. olive oil
- Parmesan cheese

Directions:
Sauté spiralized zucchini in olive oil for 4 minutes and remove from heat. Cook pasta as directed. Mix in cooked pasta into pan with zucchini, add garlic powder, salt, and Parmesan cheese to taste. Garnish with basil leaves. Serve immediately.

FRIED RICE

Who says you can't have a healthy version of fried rice that tastes amazing. Quinoa can be used in this recipe too, for added protein. Fish sauce adds a tang without making the dish taste fishy, which my kids would never stand for.

Yield: 4 servings

Ingredients
- 1 cup cooked rice (brown preferred)
- 1 extra-large organic egg
- 1 cup cooked sweet peas
- 1 tsp garlic, minced
- 1 tsp ginger, minced
- 2 tbsp. organic tamari or soy sauce
- 1 tbsp. oyster sauce or fish sauce
- 1 tbsp. organic canola oil or extra virgin olive oil
- 1 tbsp. sesame oil

Directions:
Add canola or olive oil to wok or sauté pan. Add garlic and ginger and sauté for 30 seconds on medium flame until fragrant. Add cooked peas and rice and cook for 1-2 minutes. Add tamari and fish sauce and mix well coating all of the rice, for 2 minutes. Using a spatula, move the rice to half of the pan leaving the other half of the pan empty. In that empty space cook 1 egg, breaking it into small pieces with a spatula. Mix the eggs with the rice mixture. Cook for another minute adding the sesame oil in the last few seconds.

NATANEL'S BROCCOLI CONCOCTION

My 11-year-old Natanel created this recipe and eats it at least a few days a week. It tastes better than it sounds.

Yield: 1-2 servings

Ingredients
- 2 cups broccoli steamed
- 1 tbsp. peanut butter (any nut butter would work)
- 1 tbsp. feta or other slightly salty mild white cheese, like Queso Fresco

Directions:

Wash and cut broccoli into similar size pieces to ensure all pieces cook evenly and are ready at the same time. To steam broccoli, I usually use a pan and a metal colander or a skillet. The key in both cooking methods is to add just a little bit of water, usually approx. ¼ cup and cover the pan or skillet so that steam is created without boiling the vegetable. Once the water comes to a boil, add broccoli, cover and steam for 5 minutes or to desired softness. Place steamed broccoli into serving bowl and while hot add the peanut butter and mix until peanut butter is melted. Then sprinkle cheese on top and serve immediately.

ASIAN RED CURRY TOFU

Yield: 2-4 servings

Ingredients
- 1 can unsweetened coconut milk
- 1 tbsp. red curry paste
- 2 tbsp. fish sauce or oyster sauce
- 1 tbsp. organic soy or tamari sauce
- 1 tbsp. tomato paste
- 1 cup bell pepper strips (red, yellow or green)
- 1 small zucchini sliced
- Handful mushrooms, sliced thin
- 1 pack organic fermented firm tofu
- 1 tsp organic canola oil or cold pressed extra virgin coconut or olive oil
- Basil leaves for garnish (optional)

Directions:
Cube tofu and lightly fry in wok or pan in 1 tbsp. oil and remove tofu from pan. Add coconut milk and bring to a boil over medium heat. Whisk in the red curry paste, tomato paste, fish sauce and soy sauce. Cook, stirring constantly for 2 minutes. Stir the tofu cubes into the curry sauce bringing to a gentle boil for 2- minutes. Add bell peppers, zucchini and mushrooms. Cook for an additional 3 minutes. Remove from heat and add basil.

LEMON PAPRIKA BAKED CHICKEN

Yield: 3-4 servings

Ingredients
- 6 drumsticks or 4 chicken breasts
- 2 tbsp. paprika
- Lemon juice and lemon zest (from 1 small lemon)
- 1 tsp parsley flakes
- 2 tbsp. olive oil
- 1 tsp thyme
- 1 tsp rosemary
- 1 tsp crushed garlic
- Salt and pepper to taste
- Optional variation for an Eastern flavor: add 1 tsp cumin powder and 1 tsp coriander powder

Directions:
Marinate the chicken with all the above ingredients for minimum 1 hour or in the fridge overnight. Preheat oven and bake at 350 degrees for 1 hour. Easy peazy.

SWEET AND SOUR MEATBALLS

This is a hit for the entire family; it's hard to just eat one meatball.

Yield: 4 servings

Ingredients
- 1 large onion, chopped
- 1 lb. ground organic turkey or beef (I also use half turkey, half beef to cut down on saturated fat)
- 2 organic eggs
- 2-4 tbsp. breadcrumbs* or ¼ cup cooked quinoa as gluten-free option
- 2 tbsp. arrowroot
- 1 tbsp. soup mix (MSG free)
- 2 tbsp. tamari or organic soy sauce
- 1 cup organic peach jam
- Salt and pepper to taste
- 2 tbsp. olive oil or cold pressed coconut oil

Directions:
Sauté chopped onions in skillet with oil until translucent (approximately 5 minutes) and put into a large bowl. Add turkey/beef mixture to bowl and mix. Add egg, breadcrumbs (or quinoa) and make into small balls. Fry lightly to brown both sides and drain. In separate bowl mix jam, 1 tbsp. soup mix and ½ cup warm water, 2 tbsp. tamari (or soy sauce), 2

tbsp. arrowroot. Heat jam mixture on the stove for 5 minutes on medium/low and then add meatballs, cooking for another 30 minutes or until meatballs are cooked through.

*A lot of breadcrumb products you find in grocery stores include a ton of ingredients, most of which are not very healthy for you. If you can't find one that has a few simple ingredients that you understand, you can make your own breadcrumbs quickly and easily. Just toast a couple slices of bread. Once the toast cools down, put the toast in the blender and blend to breadcrumb consistency. And voila—home-made breadcrumbs in minutes!

Nutty Yummy Fish

In general, my kids are not huge fish-lovers and have often complained that fish tastes too fishy. This recipe uses mild white fish, like cod, haddock or halibut, and tastes great.

Yield: 3-4 servings

Ingredients
- 3 tbsp. organic butter melted
- 1 lb. white wild fish (haddock, cod or halibut)
- 1/3 cup pistachios, shelled and chopped
- ½ cup almond meal
- 1 tbsp. paprika
- 2 tbsp. lemon juice
- 1 tsp garlic, minced
- 1 tsp fresh dill, chopped
- 1/8 tsp dry parsley
- 1/8 tsp onion powder
- 1 tbsp. olive oil
- Salt and pepper to taste

Directions:
In a bowl combine lemon juice, 1 tablespoon melted butter, minced garlic, dill, salt, pepper, parsley, onion powder and paprika. Marinate the fish in this mixture for at least one hour. Coat each side of the fish first in the almond meal, then

in the chopped pistachios. Preheat stovetop grill pan over medium heat, adding oil and remaining butter to the grill pan. Cook the fish for 3-5 minutes on each side. Remove fish and transfer to a platter.

Note: Exact cooking time can vary depending on the thickness of the fillet.

Tip to remove any fishiness: When you first take the fish out of its package, put it in a bowl with the juice of half a lemon and a tablespoon of salt. Let it sit in this mixture for one hour. Then rinse thoroughly with water and prepare according to recipe.

BUTTERNUT SQUASH SOUP

I love making this soup in the fall and winter.

Yield: 4 servings

Ingredients
- 20 ounces cubed butternut squash (approx. 4 cups)
- 2 onions chopped
- 2 carrots
- 1 celery stalk
- Pinch thyme
- Pinch sage
- Cilantro (a handful)
- 4 cups garbanzo beans
- 4 cups chicken or vegetable broth
- 1 tbsp. coconut oil (cold pressed)
- 1 cup light coconut milk

Directions:
Sauté vegetables in coconut oil. Add broth and boil until soft. Add 1 cup coconut milk. Simmer 20 more minutes. Blend. Eat.

Note: One medium butternut squash yields approximately 2 ½ cups.

SNACKS

Are you like me and struggle to come up with a variety of snacks to put in your kids backpack or have ready when they get home from school famished? Hope you find the list below helpful as a starting point for getting your kids to eat healthy snacks.

1. Baked tortilla chips with mango guacamole & salsa: Combine 1 mango, 2 tomatoes, 1 avocado (all diced) and juice of 1 lime. Mix ingredients and sprinkle with sea salt.
2. Natanel's broccoli concoction (see recipe on page 126)
3. Edamame with sea salt
4. Grape tomatoes with sea salt
5. Raw or cooked veggies with dip (ranch, hummus, salsa or tahini)
6. Air-popped GMO-free Popcorn
7. Nuts
8. Granola with yogurt
9. Trail mix: Mix nuts, dried cranberries, bananas, raisins and chocolate chips
10. Brown rice cake with nut butter or yogurt, sliced banana and sprinkle of cinnamon
11. Fresh fruit (grapes and clementine oranges are my kids favorite)

12. Fruit mixed in with yogurt

13. Kale chips: Toss kale in olive oil, add sea salt, then place on baking sheet, leaving room in between kale pieces, and bake on 350 degrees for 10-15 minutes or until edges are brown.

14. Baked garbanzo beans: Season the can of chickpeas (drained and rinsed) with 1 tbsp olive oil and a sprinkle of sea salt. Another variation is honey roasted where you add 1 tbsp honey to the olive oil, with a sprinkle of sea salt. Preheat oven to 400 degrees and bake chickpeas on a single layer of greased baking sheet for 30 minutes or until crunchy.

15. Pita chips and hummus

16. Pretzels with peanut or almond butter

17. Cucumber with yogurt dip (mix ½ cup plain yogurt, ½ tsp cumin, 1 tbsp chopped cilantro and 1 tbsp. chopped mint)

18. Carrots and hummus

19. Apple slices with peanut or almond butter

20. Smoothie (see recipes on pages 116-119)

DESSERT

SOFT AND MOIST CHOCOLATE CHIP COOKIES

Yield: 24 cookies

Ingredients
- 2 cups whole-wheat flour
- 1 teaspoon baking soda
- 2 eggs
- 1 tsp vanilla
- 1 cup coconut palm sugar
- 1 cup softened organic butter (unsalted)
- 1 cup chocolate chips
- 1 cup crushed nuts

Directions:
Preheat oven to 375 degrees. Mix flour and baking powder in a bowl. In a separate bowl mix brown sugar, butter, and vanilla until the mixture has a creamy consistency. Add eggs. Combine wet ingredients with the dry ingredients. Finally, mix in the chocolate chips and nuts. Spoon cookies onto greased baking sheet, keeping space between cookies as they expand while baking. Bake at 375 degrees for 10 minutes. Let cool and eat.

Banana Yogurt Sundae

My younger son, Itai, came up with this recipe (and this is the only way he'd actually eat a banana).

Yield: 1 serving

Ingredients
- 1 ripe banana chopped
- ½ cup organic vanilla yogurt
- 1 tsp organic chocolate syrup or sprinkle chocolate chips
- Organic Strawberries (or any berry)
- 1 tsp chopped nuts (optional)

Directions:
In a bowl, add chopped bananas. Pour yogurt on top of bananas. Drizzle with chocolate syrup or chocolate chips. Add sliced strawberries and top off with a sprinkle of nuts.

DECADENTLY HEALTHY CHOCOLATE PUDDING

Simple, fast and so yummy.

Yield: 1 serving

Ingredients
- 2 bananas
- 1 avocado
- 2 tbsp. cacao powder
- 2-3 tbsp. maple syrup

Directions:
Blend all until smooth and eat.

Bibliography

1. Nestle, Marion. "Ketchup Is a Vegetable? Again?" *The Atlantic*. Atlantic Media Company, 16 Nov. 2011. Web. 19 Sept. 2015.

2. Batmanghelidj, F. Your Body's Many Cries for Water: You Are Not Sick, You Are Thirsty: Don't Treat Thirst with Medications. Falls Church, VA: Global Health Solutions, 1995. Print.

3. Batmanghelidj, F. Your Body's Many Cries for Water: You Are Not Sick, You Are Thirsty.: Don't Treat Thirst with Medications. Falls Church, VA: Global Health Solutions, 1995. Print.

4. Batmanghelidj, M.D., F. "Frequently Asked Questions." *WaterCure*. N.p., n.d. Web. 19 Sept. 2015.

5. Merriam-Webster. Merriam-Webster, n.d.Web. 19 Sept. 2015.

6. "Most Bottled Water Brands Don't Disclose Information About Source, Purity and Contaminants." EWG. Environmental Working Group, 7 July 2009. Web. 19 Sept. 2015

7. Zeratsky, Katherine, R.D., L.D. "Nutrition and Healthy Eating." What Is BPA? Should I Be Worried about It? Mayo Clinic, n.d. Web. 19 Sept. 2015.

8. "Don't Brush Teeth After Eating Acidic Foods - Bellevue Dentist." *Bellevue Dental Care*. N.p., 27 May 2015.Web. 19 Sept.2015.

9. "Frequently Asked Questions About Sugar." *Frequently Asked* Questions About Sugar. American Heart Associ tion,19May2014.Web.11Oct.2015.<http://www.heart. org/HEARTORG/GettingHealthy/Nutrition-Center/HealthyDietGoals/Frequently-Asked-Questions-About Sugar_UCM_306725_Article.jsp>.

10. *Estimated Calorie Needs per Day by Age, Gender, and Physical Activity Level.* (n.d.): n. pag. *United States Department of Agriculture.* Web. 18 Sept. 2105. <http://www.cnpp.usda.gov/ sites/default/files/usda_food_patterns/Estimated-CalorieNeedsPerDayTable.pdf>.

11. Donovan, Travis. "Pesticides In Food: What To Eat And What To Avoid (PHOTOS)." *The Huffington Post.* TheHuffingtonPost.com, 25 May 2011. Web. 11 Oct. 2015.<http://www.huffing-tonpost.com/2010/05/20/pesticides-in-food-what-t_n_581937.html>.

12. "GMO Defined." GMO Awareness. GMO-Awareness.com, 29 Apr. 2011. Web. 12 Oct. 2015. <http://gmo-awareness.com/all-about-gmos/gmo-defined/>.

13. Zeratsky, Katherine, R.D., L.D. "Nutrition and Healthy Eating."*Monosodium Glutamate (MSG): Is It Harmful?* Mayo Clinic, n.d. Web. 23 Sept. 2015. <http://www.mayoclinic.org/healthy-lifestyle/nutrition-and-healthy-eating/expert-answers/monosodium-glutamate/faq-20058196>.

14. Downs, Martin, MPH. "The Truth about 7 Common Food Additives." WebMD. WebMD, 17 Dec. 2008. Web. 19 Sept. 2015. <http://www.webmd.com/diet/the-truth-about-seven-common-food-additives?page=1>.

15. "The Feingold Diet Program for ADHD." *The Feingold Diet Program for ADHD.* Feingold Association of the United States (FAUS), 2015. Web. 12 Oct. 2015. <http://www.feingold.org/>.

16. Schonwald, A. "ADHD and Food Additives Revisited." *AAP Grand Rounds*19.2 (2008): 17. Web.

17. Andrews, David. "EWG's Food Scores Just Took the Work out of Grocery Shopping for Me." EWG's Food Scores. Environmental Working Group, n.d. Web. 19 Sept.2015.<http://www.ewg.org/foodscores/content/natural-vs-artificial-flavors>.

18. CFR - Code of Federal Regulations Title 21." CFR - Code of Federal Regulations Title 21. U.S. Food & Drug Administration, 21 Aug. 2015. Web. 19 Sept. 2015.

19. Hari, Vani. "FOOD BABE TV: Do You Eat Beaver Butt?" *Food Babe.* Food Babe, 09 Sept. 2013. Web. 27 Sept. 2015. <http://foodbabe.com/2013/09/09/food-babe-tv-do-you-eat-beaver-butt/#more-14529>.

20. "Carrageenan." Cornucopia Institute (n.d.): n. pag. Mar. 2013. Web. 19 Sept. 2015.

21. Epstein, Samuel S., M.D. "What's in Your Milk? An Expose on the DANGERS of Genetically Engineered

Milk." *What's in Your Milk? An Expose on the DAN-GERS of Genetically Engineered Milk.* Organic Consumers Association, 3 Jan. 2007. Web. 19 Sept. 2015. <https://www.organicconsumers.org/news/whats-your-milk-expose-dangers-genetically-engineered-milk>.

22. "Meat and Poultry Labeling Terms." Meat and Poultry Labeling Terms. United States Department of Agriculture, 10 Aug. 2015. Web. 19 Sept. 2015. <http://www.fsis.usda.gov/wps/portal/fsis/topics/food-safety-education/get-answers/food-safety-fact-sheets/food-labeling/meat-and-poultry-labeling-terms/meat-and-poultry-labeling-terms.

23. "Animals Used for Free-Range and Organic Meat." *PETA Animals Used for Free Range and Organic Meat Comments.* PETA, n.d. Web. 20 Sept. 2015. <http://www.peta.org/issues/animals-used-for-food/organic-free-range-meat/>.

24. Roizman, Tracey. "Do Hormones in the Food Supply Affect the Human Body?" Healthy Eating. SF Gate, n.d. Web. 01 Nov. 2015. <http://healthyeating.sfgate.com/hormones-food-supply-affect-human-body-2194.html>.

25. "List of Names for Artificial Sweeteners." *List of Names for Artificial Sweeteners.* The Dr. Oz Show, 7 Mar. 2014. Web. 12 Oct. 2015.<http://www.doctoroz.com/article/list-names-artificial-sweeteners>.

26. Nall, Rachel. "Daily Sugar Recommendations for Kids." *LIVESTRONG.COM*. LIVESTRONG.COM, 23 Apr. 2015. Web. 20 Sept. 2015. <http://www.livestrong.com/article/458552-how-much-sugar-per-day-for-kids/>.

27. *WESTBROOK, JULIA. "19 Ways To Give Up Sugar."* Rodale's Organic Life. Rodale's Organic Life, 11 Sept. 2015. Web. 20 Sept.2015.<http://www.rodalesorgani-clife.com/wellbein/19-ways-give sugar?cid=Soc_Facebook_RealSimple _0915&xid=soc_socialflow_facebook_realsimple>.

28. Sandle, Tim. "Excess Fat And Sugar Can Lead To Cognitive Decline - The Latest News." *The Latest News*. N.p., 24 June 2015. Web. 20 Sept. 2015. <http://www.thelatestnews.com/excess-fat-sugar-can-lead-cognitive-decline/>.

29. Hari, Vani. "Food Babe Investigates - Chipotle Ingredients Now Available."*Food Babe*. N.p., 24 Mar. 2013. Web. 21 Sept. 2015. <http://food-babe.com/2013/03/24/a-food-babe-investigates-win-chipotle-posts-ingredients/>.

30. "EWG's Shopper's Guide to Pesticides in Produce™." *EWG's 2015 Shopper's Guide to Pesticides in Produce.*™ Environmental Working Group, n.d. Web. 20 Sept. 2015. <http://www.ewg.org/food-news/?gclid=CjwKEAjwsvmvBRCT5ozK-dmY7D4SJACyIoJmo7pix3C3aY4gbxz-tH4HOKswUa2ZzoRBHorytAWY-hoC1Bjw_wcB>.

31. Lemeric, Wendy. "Swedish Family Participating In Study Eats Organic Food For Two Weeks [WATCH VIDEO]." *International Business Times AU*. N.p., 13 May 2015. Web. 20 Sept. 2015. <http://www.ibtimes.com.au/swedish-family-participating-study-eats-organic-food-two-weeks-watch-video-1447895>.

32. Grussi, Rachel. "| GaiamTV." *Gaiam TV*. N.p., 3 Mar. 2014. Web. 12 Oct. 2015. <http://www.gaiamtv.com/article/5-colors-phyto-nutrients-eat-rainbow>.

33. Katz, David, and Catherine Katz. "Nutrition Detectives." *A Katz & Katz Production Family Edition* (2009): n. pag. Katz & Katz Production, 31 Mar. 2009. Web. 18 Sept. 2015.<http://www.turnthetidefoundation.org/NDmaterials/ND_Family_edition.pdf>.

34. "Build Healthy Kids | Nutrition 101 | The Basics Made Simple." *Build Healthy Kids | Nutrition 101 | The Basics Made Simple*. N.p., n.d. Web. 27 Sept. 2015. <http://www.buildhealthykids.com/genrequire-ments.html

35. Laskowski, Edward R., M.D. "Fitness." Exercise: How Much Do I Need Every Day? Mayo Clinic, 3 Jan. 2014. Web. 01 Nov. 2015. <http://www.mayoclinic.org/healthy-lifestyle/fitness/expert-answers/exercise/faq-20057916>.

36. Alyssa Sparacino, Alyssa. "11 Surprising Health Benefits of Sleep."*Health.com*. N.p., n.d. Web. 13 Oct.

2015. <http://www.health.com/health/gal-lery/0,,20459221,00.html.

37. Max Hirshkowitz, PhD, Kaitlyn Whiton, Steven M. Albert, PhD, Cathy Alessi, MD, Oliviero Bruni, MD, Lydia DonCarlos, PhD, Nancy Hazen, PhD, John Herman, PhD, Eliot S. Katz, MD, Leila Kheirandish-Gozal, MD, MSc, David N. Neubauer, MD, Anne E. O'Donnell, MD, Maurice Ohayon, MD, DSc, PhD, John Peever, PhD, Robert Rawding, PhD, Ramesh C. Sachdeva, MD, PhD, JD, Belinda Setters, MD, Michael V. Vitiello, PhD, J. Catesby Ware, PhD, Paula J. Adams Hillard, MD. "National Sleep Foundation's Sleep Time Duration Recommendations: Methodology and Results Summary." *Journal of the National Sleep Foundation* 1.1 (2015): 40-43. Web. 25 Sept. 2015. <http://www.sleephealthjournal.org/article/S2352-7218 (15)00015-7/abstract>.

38. Sutherland, Stephani. "Bright Screens Could Delay Bedtime." *Scientific American Global RSS*. N.p., 19 Dec. 2012. Web. 25 Sept. 2015. <http://www.scientificamerican.com/article/bright-screens-could-delay-bedtime/>.

39. "Gratitude." Gratitude: Definition of Gratitude in Oxford Dictionary (American English) (US). Oxford, n.d. Web. 01 Nov. 2015. <http://www.oxforddictionaries.com/us/definition/american_english/gratitude>.

40. Forleo, Maria. "All About the inside Scoop." *RSS*. Maria Forleo, 2015. Web. 13 Oct. 2015.

<http://www.marieforleo.com/about/the-company/>.

41. Weil M.D., Andrew. "Videos." *Dr. Weil's Breathing Exercises: 4-7-8 Breath*. Weil Lifestyle, 2015. Web. 13 Oct. 2015.
<http://www.drweil.com/drw/u/VDR00160/Dr-Weils-Breathing-Exercises-4-7-8-Breath.html>.

Acknowledgments

I would like to express my deepest gratitude to the special people who saw me through this book. I never imagined I'd be writing a book. The outpour of positive feedback has been unbelievable and very inspiring.

I'd like to thank my husband Eli, who is my soulmate and my rock. Thank you for always inspiring me and supporting me in pursuing my dreams. I love you.

To my boys, Natanel and Itai, who without you, this book wouldn't exist, since I only found my passion in life through being your mom. You both taught me the meaning of unconditional love and I want to make you proud of me every day that I can. My wish is that by learning the lessons in this book, you will better your lives and the lives of those around you. My hope is that you will teach them to your kids (my grandkids!), and so on...

To Natalie – my sister, my first best friend and my toughest critic, always pushing me beyond my limits and my comfort zone, because you always saw in me what I've just come to understand recently. I can't imagine doing anything meaningful without you.

To my brother Robert who always has my back through thick and thin: Thank you.

To my parents who raised me to be a strong, independent woman who is not a quitter or intimidated by the hard work and discipline it takes to reach your goals: Thank you.

To Isabel, who has been instrumental in editing this book. It has been such a special experience working on this project with you and getting closer to you during this process.

To my kids babysitter and partner in crime, Fareeda, who tirelessly tries to make sure my kids eat healthy so that they can give everything else their all. My whole family sees you as part of our family and appreciates and thanks you.

To Bridget for always being my biggest fan and great supporter throughout this process. To D'Pals (Dena, Pearl & Amanda) for always believing in me despite all the craziness around us. And to all my great mommy-friends, Joanna, Holly, Jen, Rivka and Tammy, who took the time to read this entire book and give me great feedback so that I could make it a better book for all of you.

To the Institute for Integrative Nutrition for an amazing health education that has forever changed my life. I always had a passion for health but through the unbelievable support of IIN, I was able to learn from some of the world's top health and wellness experts which equipped me with extensive knowledge in holistic nutrition, health coaching, and preventive health.

To all the amazing activists and teachers out there who inspire me to better myself and teach others—John and Ocean Robbins, Vani Hari, Dr. Mark Hyman, Dr. Andrew Weil, Dr. David Katz, Gabrielle Bernstein, Kris Carr, Marie Farleo, Deepak Chopra, Oprah Winfrey and many more.

To Create Space and Amazon, thank you so much for all your support and patience during the publishing process.

And finally to all the kids out there... If any of what I've written in this book can help them have a better shot at a healthier, happier life then I have accomplished my ultimate goal – to focus on healing children.

Index

ABOUT THE AUTHOR

Lilly Cadoch is a certified Integrative Nutrition health coach living in New York with her husband Eli, her two boys Natanel and Itai, and her dog, Angel. She has spent the last few years learning about nutrition and mindful living for both herself and her family while working full time at an advertising agency in NYC. She has a passion for food and cooking and loves spending time in the kitchen experimenting with different recipes with her kids. She spends her time educating herself on various different aspects of food and nutrition, creating life memories with her kids, going to spin class with her husband, and playing in her backyard garden.

For more information: www.BusyMomsCheatSheet.com

Cheat Sheet Notes:

Cheat Sheet Notes:

CPSIA information can be obtained
at www.ICGtesting.com
Printed in the USA
LVOW13s1610010317
525811LV00010B/765/P